To Build Christ's Kingdom

Other titles in the *Canterbury Studies in Spiritual Theology* series:

Glory Descending: Michael Ramsey and His Writings
Edited by Douglas Dales, Geoffrey Rowell, John Habgood and Rowan Williams

The Truth-Seeking Heart: An Austin Farrer Reader
Edited by Ann Loades and Robert MacSwain

Firmly I Believe: An Oxford Movement Reader
Edited by Raymond Chapman

Forthcoming:

The Sacramental Life: A Gregory Dix Reader
Edited by Simon Jones

Holiness and Happiness: A Traherne Reader
Edited by Denise Inge

Canterbury Studies in Spiritual Theology

To Build Christ's Kingdom

F. D. Maurice and His Writings

Edited and Introduced by
Jeremy Morris

Canterbury
Press
Norwich

First published in 2007 by the Canterbury Press Norwich
(a publishing imprint of Hymns Ancient & Modern Limited,
a registered charity)
9–17 St Alban's Place, London N1 0NX

www.scm-canterburypress.co.uk

British Library Cataloguing in Publication data

A catalogue record for this book is available
from the British Library

ISBN 978-1-85311-777-0

Typeset by Regent Typesetting, London
Printed and bound in Great Britain by
William Clowes Ltd, Beccles, Suffolk

Contents

Acknowledgments

The compilation of this reader of F. D. Maurice texts has been a welcome addition to some years of work on his theology that has issued in various academic publications of mine – welcome, because I hope it will bring Maurice's name and writing to a wider readership than that of the theological and historical journals. Maurice deserves still to be read by all interested in the history and also in the future of Anglicanism. But this book would not have come into being without the support and encouragement of several people. I would especially like to thank Christine Smith, the commissioning editor at SCM-Canterbury Press, for her initiative, interest and forbearance. I would also like to thank Dan Hardy, Tim Jenkins, Chris Williams, Graham Howes and John Nurser for their interest and support over the period this was prepared, as well as the Master and Fellows of Trinity Hall for allowing me study leave to complete it. Inevitably my personal debt to my family – to Alex, and to Isobel, William and Ursula – comes before all else. Without them, I'm not sure any of this would have been possible. This book is dedicated to my father, David, a lifelong Anglican and admirer of the *Prayer Book*.

Abbreviations

CDOS	*Christmas Day and other Sermons* (1843)
DS	*The Doctrine of Sacrifice* (2nd edn, reprinted 1893)
GKH	*The Gospel of the Kingdom of Heaven* (2nd edn, 1893)
KC, 1st edn	*The Kingdom of Christ* (1st edn, 1838)
KC, 2nd edn	*The Kingdom of Christ* (2nd edn, 1842; 4th edn, 1891, used here)
Life	F. Maurice, *Life and Letters of F. D. Maurice* (2nd edn, 1884)
PBLP	*The Prayer-Book and the Lord's Prayer* (1880 edn)
PFP	*Politics for the People* (1848)
PKOT	*Prophets and Kings of the Old Testament* (3rd edn, 1871)
RFNJPC	*Reasons for Not Joining a Party in the Church* (1st edn, 1841)
Sermons	*Sermons*, First Series (2nd edn, 1860)
SNB	*Subscription No Bondage* (1835)
TE	*Theological Essays* (4th edn, 1881)
TGSJ	*The Gospel of St John* (2nd edn, 1878)
TLRWP	*Three Letters to the Revd. William Palmer* (2nd edn, 1842)
WR	*What is Revelation?* (1st edn, 1859)

Part 1

Introduction: Maurice's Life and Work

Introduction

Who are the great theologians and spiritual writers of the Anglican tradition of Christianity? Most people, I expect, would be hard-pressed to answer that question. Lutherans have Luther to whom they can appeal, Calvinists have John Calvin, Methodists have John and Charles Wesley, and Roman Catholics of course have their own great tradition of thinkers. But Anglicans have always been a little coy about naming great forerunners, partly because they have been suspicious of attributing too much importance to one or two leading figures, and partly perhaps because they have been at pains to emphasize their common inheritance with the great theologians and spiritual writers of the medieval Church and the Church of the early centuries. That has made it somewhat awkward to suggest that Anglicanism has been shaped decisively by particular people in the modern era, because Anglicans have wanted to stress that their churches are part of the great, historic stream of Christian belief. Delve a little into the history of the Anglican churches, however, and various names do come to the fore as having wielded an exceptional influence on the theology and spirituality of Anglicanism – names like Thomas Cranmer (1489–1556), Richard Hooker (c.1554–1600), Lancelot Andrewes (1555–1626), William Wilberforce (1759–1833), John Keble (1792–1866), Evelyn Underhill (1875–1941), William Temple (1881–1944), Gregory Dix (1901–52), Austin Farrer (1904–68) and Michael Ramsey (1904–88).

All of these people – many of whom feature in this series – have played an important role in moulding the theology and practice of Anglicanism over the centuries. But no such list would be complete without the name of F. D. Maurice (1805–72). His influence on modern Anglicanism has been remarkable. He has exercised a central role in the shaping of Anglican attitudes towards the theology of ministry, social responsibility, the doctrine of the atonement, ideas of heaven and hell, the doctrines of the Incarnation and the Trinity, and church unity and ecumenical method, to name but a few subjects with which he was concerned. The scope of his influence was immense. He is credited by many with having founded, in effect, the modern tradition of liberal Anglicanism, and though he disliked being labelled as a 'liberal', it is true that many of the most characteristic features of liberal or 'central' Anglican opinion in the twentieth and twenty-first centuries can be traced back to him, if not necessarily as their originator, nevertheless as one of their most creative and original voices. But in many respects he was a traditional High Churchman, and yet one who also had a profound respect for Evangelicalism. His influence came to permeate the whole of the Anglican tradition, particularly in Anglican approaches to ecumenism, and in the development of social theology.

Many Anglicans characteristically talk about their Church as 'comprehensive', by which they mean that it includes within itself a wide range of different theological opinion, from 'Conservative Evangelical' to 'Anglo-Catholic', and yet all too often they are unaware that the great theologian of this idea of 'comprehensiveness' was F. D. Maurice. He was concerned above all to persuade his fellow Christians to avoid the sins of narrowness and exclusiveness, not because he held simply a secular ideal of tolerance, but because he was convinced that passionately-held and genuine principles lay at the root of church conflict. The breadth of Christian truth, which always lies beyond the individual capacity of men and women to express it in all its richness and depth, encompassed the truths for which church people of different parties were contending. The Church of England witnessed to the universality, the Catholicity, of the Church of England in its objective features, its sacraments, its ministry, its liturgy, its standard of faith – that is the High Churchman in Maurice speaking. But it would be irreparably damaged if, for example, it were to lose its Evangelical wing, with its forthright advocacy of evangelical truth. In expressing himself in this way, Maurice was laying out for his fellow Anglicans – and indeed for other Christian believers – an implicit vision of Christian unity, for all Christians were called in the Church to try to rekindle the original breadth and force of the Christian gospel, and to re-knit the great divisions of the Christian Church, caused by the quarrels of Christian against Christian in the past, in a future great, united Church. Maurice, then, gave his countrymen a key to interpreting the Christian past that was even-handed in its application, and yet which served as a subtle and persuasive Anglican apologetic.

And yet his name is almost unknown today. In his lifetime, he published over 5 million words. Books poured from him, the product of a lifetime's teaching and preaching. They were almost all written in the service of the Church of England, since they were usually devised as sermons for the particular congregations he served. He was held in high regard by a wide circle of people, including many of the great Victorian men and women of letters – Alfred Tennyson, Thomas Carlyle, George Eliot, Mrs Gaskell, Charlotte Brontë, William Gladstone, Thomas Hughes, Charles Kingsley, and Octavia Hill were among his admirers, to name but a few. His preaching drew a devoted following when he was Chaplain at Lincoln's Inn. His work was dense and packed with ideas. Even the modern reader who is fully aware of the subsequent history of Anglican theology will still find enormously stimulating passages in his work. And yet, today, his books are largely unpublished. His literary style can seem ponderous to the reader accustomed to 'sound bites'. It is certainly demanding. Sentences full of multiple sub-clauses sometimes stretch over a page or more. He addresses great sequences of rhetorical questions to his audience. Precious insights are often wrapped up in a tortured, allusive prose. That is why a 'Reader' of key Maurice texts, such as this book, is long overdue. I hope it will bring before you not only extracts from some of the most significant books of Anglican theology to be published in the nineteenth century, but something of the depth and subtlety of this most extraordinary of Anglicans.

A short biography

John Frederick Denison Maurice was born on 29 August 1805 to a Unitarian father and mother. He almost never used 'John' in later life, and was known simply as 'F. D. Maurice' by most people, or as 'Fred' by his sisters. 'Unitarian' is something of a catch-all term that covered a wide range of belief in this period. Many Unitarians denied the doctrine of Christ's divinity, and so also denied the doctrine of the Trinity. Others, such as Maurice's father, were much more conventional in their beliefs, and tended to be agnostic about Christ's divinity, but were happy to use Trinitarian formulae. Unitarianism was generally a progressive, liberal form of belief, suspicious of establishment Anglicanism. But in Maurice's youth, his mother and sisters abandoned Unitarianism for a rigid Calvinist Evangelicalism. His father, a minister, never willingly accepted their change. Family division over religion scarred Maurice's upbringing, and surely helped to foster his deep desire for Christian unity. Briefly influenced by his sisters' Calvinism, he moved beyond it, however, through an appreciation of the work of the Scottish lay theologian Thomas Erskine (1788–70), a near-contemporary with whom he later became friendly. He read law at Cambridge, where he came under the spell of Julius Hare (whose sister he was to marry), later Archdeacon and a spirited Anglican controversialist, through whom he absorbed the influence of the poet and thinker Samuel Taylor Coleridge. From Coleridge, Maurice learnt the merit of appreciating the complex nature of truth, and its many-sidedness. No one opinion or point of view could claim to capture truth completely. The task of the theologian was to explore the complementary truthful insights embedded in apparently conflicting schools of thought within Christianity. Yet Maurice also moved, like Coleridge himself, towards mainstream Anglican belief. In 1831, after a further spell of study at Oxford, he was baptized as an Anglican, and finally in 1834 ordained into the ministry of the established Church.

Maurice's life was not to be, in outward essentials, a particularly dramatic one. After a brief curacy at Bubbenhall in Warwickshire, he was appointed Chaplain of Guy's Hospital. His first published theological work was a short pamphlet, *Subscription no Bondage* (1835), which defended the principle of subscription to the Thirty-Nine Articles at Oxford University, and won the admiration of leading members of the Oxford Movement. The position at Guy's, despite its demanding pastoral work, gave Maurice further scope to develop his theological writing, and it was there that he wrote his most famous book, *The Kingdom of Christ* (1838). His appointment to the newly-established King's College, London, as Professor in English Literature and History in 1840 reflected the perception of him as an original, but relatively conservative, voice, and it gave him a secure teaching base, consolidated in 1846 when he was appointed Professor of Theology in the new theological college at King's. In the same year, he took up simultaneously the position of Chaplain of Lincoln's Inn. His dual vocation, as theologian and minister, was now well established. In a growing list of publications, he began to mark out a distinctive position in Anglican controversy. He criticized the partisanship of some Evangelicals and Tractarians, and – in *Reasons for not Joining a Party in the Church* (1841) – urged his fellow Anglicans to avoid the temptation to take sides in the heightening tension between them. In the same year, in his *Three Letters to the Revd. William Palmer*, he strongly supported the scheme for a joint Anglican-Lutheran bishopric at Jerusalem, which drew the ire of many of the Tractarians. But his views were always somewhat idiosyncratic, and his encouragement of the movement, begun in 1848, that eventually came to be called 'Christian Socialism', and controversy over his attempt to reinterpret the doctrine of eternal life in his *Theological Essays*, led to his forced resignation from King's in 1853. This was a severe blow, from which his reputation in the Church of England at large took many years to recover. His ministry at Lincoln's Inn continued, however, as did the educational projects with which he was now associated, such as the Working Men's College. He relinquished Lincoln's Inn and took up the position of priest-in-charge of St Peter's, Vere Street, in 1860, despite some opposition from London Evangelical clergy.

But in the 1860s, his gradual rehabilitation began. Partly through the influence of his great friend and disciple Charles Kingsley, he was appointed to the Knightbridge Chair of Casuistry, Moral Theology and Moral Philosophy at Cambridge University in 1866, and the familiar pattern of pastoral charge conjointly with academic responsibility was repeated when he also took up the position of Vicar-Chaplain of St Edward's, Cambridge, a position in effect in the gift of his old college, Trinity Hall. Almost uninterrupted by the storms of controversy he faced in the 1850s was his astonishing literary output, and even as his health began to fail in 1871 he was still writing. He died on 1 April 1872 at his nieces' house in London, where he had been taken to be nursed in mid-March.

A spiritual tradition

The Anglicanism of Maurice's day was a religious tradition in a state of flux. At the beginning of the nineteenth century it was hardly conceived as a distinct tradition, in the sense that it could be compared with Lutheranism or the Reformed churches. No one talked of Anglicanism as an 'ism'. It was simply the religion of the established Church in England, Wales and Ireland. It had been exported overseas by the process of colonial expansion. But as yet there was no real consciousness of an Anglican Communion as such. Apart from the United States, where independence had forced Anglicans to break from the jurisdiction of the Church of England and create their own network of new dioceses (seeking ordination from bishops in the minority Episcopal Church in Scotland), the colonial Anglican churches were directly under the Church of England. The Church of England was widely seen as a Protestant church that had (in its own understanding) providentially retained the threefold order of bishops, priests and deacons. Central to its self-understanding was its role as a state church. Religious toleration had been granted in England at the end of the seventeenth century, but it was grudging and limited.

But in the course of the nineteenth century, much of this changed. A series of crises in Church–State relations led to the withering of much of the establishment privilege of the Church of England. Gradually, overseas, semi-autonomous (and later fully autonomous) Anglican provinces came into being. Moreover, internally Anglicans became caught up in a complicated process of doctrinal division and definition. First, the Evangelical movement sought renewal of the Church from within, after the loss of John Wesley's Methodist movement from the Church in the late eighteenth century. But, partly in reaction to the loss of the traditional links between Church and State, and partly in reaction to what they took to be the Evangelicals' disparagement of the sacramental traditions of Anglicanism, High Churchmen in turn – under the influence in particular of the Oxford Movement – began to define what *they* meant by 'Anglican' much more closely than ever before. This developing 'two party' conflict between Evangelicals and Tractarians was further complicated by the emergence of a further 'party', a 'Broad Church' group who wanted to defend the national vocation of the Church of England, and accordingly emphasized its theological breadth.

In Maurice's own lifetime, then, the notion of what it might mean to be an Anglican was undergoing profound change. In the confusion of church party conflict, there was a danger that any sense of unity and identity in the Anglican churches might be lost, and that one group or other would seek to dominate the Church and drive out all others. Maurice's contribution to the consolidation of Anglicanism as a distinct spiritual tradition within worldwide Christianity was to point both to the objective features of the Anglican churches – especially their retention of what would come to be called 'Catholic order', and their historic relationship with the nation – and to value the specific spiritual insights of Evangelicalism, Liberalism or the Broad Church, and High Churchmanship. From Coleridge, he had drawn the realization that human apprehension of religious truth is proximate, and partial. Whenever someone claims to know the whole truth – to represent exclusively the true spirit of the gospel – we are entitled to be sceptical. There is always much to be learned from others who profess to follow Christ and yet seem different from us. Yet despite all the many differences between Christians, what makes it possible to have trust in the faith we have received within the Anglican churches is the very fact that there is something objective, something that stands beyond individual opinion in the very history and character of these churches. Their structure is itself a witness to their Catholicity. The Church of England's faithfulness to the gospel was reflected in its unity, and to the extent that

Anglicans fell foul of what Maurice called the 'sin of separation', the sectarian temptation to exalt just one opinion over others, they risked the loss of that faithfulness. Maurice's understanding of Anglicanism, then, was rooted in historic institutions, and yet it encompassed diversity and change within itself.

The Church and the Kingdom

In order to grasp in more detail the highly original character of Maurice's thought, it is necessary now to turn to look more closely at several key points in his life. First, and of most lasting consequence, was the writing of his great work, *The Kingdom of Christ*. Maurice embraced the Church of England at one of its greatest periods of crisis (it is perhaps encouraging to beleaguered Anglicans today to reflect on this), when its resistance to political reform exposed its vulnerability. It was, in the years following the granting of political rights to Dissenters and Roman Catholics in 1828 and 1829, intimately associated with the governing elite. The local magistracy had a high proportion of clerical appointees. Clergy practically everywhere were members of the gentry. They were not necessarily rich, however. Many, in fact, were poor, and could only offset the low income of a benefice, in an age long before national stipends, by garnering up two or more appointments simultaneously. 'Pluralism', as this was called, looked corrupt, even if it was for some a practical necessity. The inequalities of wealth, and the inefficiency of the established Church, along with its legal privileges, were highlighted by political radicals, and by Dissenting critics. In the end, the sting of all this was removed by church reform – but not before the Church of England had passed through a time of bitter conflict and criticism.

Maurice knew very well what he was embracing when he contemplated entering the Church's ministry. '[As] an establishment it will be overturned, I know not how soon, I am nearly convinced', he wrote to his perplexed father, and 'yet I would rather be a member of it now than in the days of its greatest prosperity.'[1] For a short while he was associated with the movement of vigorous High Church revival we now call the Oxford Movement. He was wooed unsuccessfully by John Henry Newman and Edward Pusey for the position of Professor of Political Economy (though he knew next to nothing about the subject). But a decisive break with them came in 1836 when he read Pusey's views on baptism, which mistakenly he assumed to represent a doctrine of 'salvation by baptism'. In fact, though Maurice remained in many ways an orthodox High Churchman, his abiding theological preoccupations were strikingly different from those of the Oxford Movement.

In 1837, by now Chaplain to Guy's Hospital in London, Maurice began an 'answer' to Pusey, cast ostensibly as a series of letters to a Quaker friend. These were eventually published in book form as his most famous contribution to Anglican theology, *The Kingdom of Christ*. To the modern reader, it is a complex and rather uneven book. Moments of extraordinary clarity and brilliance are buried in cumbersome paragraphs. Moreover, the basic structure of the book is somewhat disconnected. It feels like three books rolled up into one – a selective historical discussion of Christian division, a treatise on the visible marks of the Church, and a defence of elements of the Church of England. Yet, for all that, the book represented a remarkable application of Coleridge's dialectical method to the Anglican understanding of the Church. It signalled certain basic lines of approach that – naturally with much modification – eventually were to become vital to modern Anglican ecclesiology.

Maurice's analysis of the history of Christian disunity began from a key question: 'Where can we find the Catholic Church?' But instead of defining Catholicity in the abstract, and then finding the Church that conforms to it, Maurice assumed the inherent Catholicity of all the major branches of Protestantism, and sought to draw out how it might be identified. In the case of Quakerism, for example, he drew attention to its doctrine of the 'inner light', and in the case of Lutheranism and Reformed Christianity (which together he calls 'Pure Protestantism') to justification through faith alone, the supreme authority of Scripture, and the doctrine of divine election. He even sought to emphasize positively the Unitarian yearning after unity. Yet in each case – most seriously in Unitarianism – these 'positive principles' had become embedded in misleading, self-assertive doctrinal developments. The authentic history of the separated churches of Protestantism yielded Christian truth in many different Christian communities, but also an equal share of responsibility for conflict and division.

To Maurice, then, the history of Christendom was a fragmented one, a descent into rigidified theological 'systems' and sects, within which, nevertheless, the Catholicity of the Church could still be found, even in a dispersed form. God, Maurice was saying, continued to be present with and in his Church in all its desperate divisions. And so Maurice's providential reading of the Church's history directed him towards a theological rehabilitation of the idea of Christian unity. His hermeneutic of Catholicity, applied in such a way as to demonstrate the persistence of the Church in all churches and sects which professed the Triune name despite the increasing fragmentation and sectarianism of Western Christendom, enabled him to reconceive the unity of the Christian Church beyond the exclusive ecclesiological emphases of the Catholicism and Protestantism of his day.

He dealt directly with Roman Catholicism and the Church of England in the second main part of the book. Here he explored six 'signs' of Catholicity – baptism, Eucharist, Scripture, creeds, the apostolic ministry, and liturgical tradition. Take out liturgical tradition, and you have in essence the main points of what was later to become the Lambeth Quadrilateral – the four-fold basis on which Anglicans seek unity with other churches. Now, however, his method changed tack. Instead of the finely-balanced assessment of positive principle and negative development that we saw at work in the first part of the book, here each of the signs was described as it was found in the Church of England, and then its corruption depicted in the case of Roman Catholicism. Most readers find Maurice's treatment of Roman Catholicism particularly unsatisfactory, and it is true that he was not exactly a sympathetic or informed observer. His natural affinities, despite his broadly High Church understanding of the sacraments and the ministry, lay with Protestantism.

Yet it is the third main part of the book that raises most questions for readers today. Here, Maurice turned his attention directly to the Church of England. He applied the same dialectical logic used in the first part of the book to the internal divisions of the Church. In each of the main 'parties' – Evangelical, Liberal and Catholic – again he found both positive principles and misleading development. By implication, the Anglican Church was greater than the mere sum of its parts. It needed each of the main parties, yet it needed to rise above their conflict. This was the root of the argument for the 'comprehensiveness' of the Church of England with which Maurice's name has become indelibly associated. He marked out a vision of church unity that applied as forcefully to his own Church as it did to relations between separated churches. And yet, we should be careful not to assume that Maurice was propounding a new 'theory'. His method depended on an assumption of historical analysis, and amounted to an argument for a historical ecclesiology. He did not try to defend the Church of England from first principles, so much as seek to understand the Church as he found it historically existing.

But this did leave his argument vulnerable, on several counts. He seemed unaware of the sophistication of analysis required to discern the positive principles in their corrupt or distorted setting in history. Though his argument was historical, he was not a subtle historian, and his account of history left much to be desired. At times, for all its originality of insight, his argument looked sketchy and incomplete. He gave many hostages to fortune, in the form of misleading generalizations and selectivity of evidence. Moreover, he was not always alert to the weaknesses of some of the assumptions he made. This is particularly true with regard to his dependence on the principle of nationality, which he used to defend the establishment of the Church of England, but which he took in a spirit that owed much to Romantic ideas of intrinsic national character. The English, he thought, were a practical and politically-astute people. The mixed nature of the English Church suited this national character. Nations were a divinely-ordained provision, along with the family and the Church, and so the English Church represented the true form of Christian community for the nation. Maurice's apparent ecumenical sympathies were somewhat undermined by the national argument.

Yet *The Kingdom of Christ*, for all its faults, remains a great book, of lasting significance for Anglicanism. Its particular value is twofold. First, in it the genesis of modern ecumenical method can be discerned. At the time Maurice was writing, relations between Anglicans and other churches, Protestant as well as Catholic, were fraught with tension and sometimes hostility. Dissenters were seen as schismatics, Catholics as sinister and 'unEnglish'. Maurice's retrieval of the 'positive principles' of separated churches, through his historical exploration of the emergence of their doctrinal traditions, in due course was to become widely imitated as a way of appreciating more sympathetically the history of churches other than our own. Second, the argument from 'comprehensiveness', for all its evident weaknesses, became a vital tool for Anglicans as they sought to understand how it was possible for a church so apparently divided in principle and practice to remain one. By attaching significance in particular to the possession of the 'signs' of the Catholic Church, Maurice could affirm the Catholicity of the Church of England, at the same time as acknowledging regretfully its internal conflicts over the interpretation of doctrine. And yet, on his view, the 'signs' were not merely human artefacts; they were intrinsically powerful symbols and expressions of divine realities. 'Here is a theologian', Michael Ramsey was to write, 'whose emphasis upon Church order springs directly from his sense of the Gospel of God.'[2]

Human being and human society

Underlying this vision of the Church lay a particular understanding of the nature of human society, and in turn a particular understanding of the doctrine of creation. Maurice's views on this count were fixed very early on, by his early thirties, and remained unchanged until his death. They reflect the influence of Platonic philosophy on him, an influence he imbibed partly through his Unitarian background, and partly from studying Plato at Cambridge. Some scholars have gone so far as to accuse him of subordinating the Christian revelation to Platonism, but this is unfair.[3] Maurice always assumed the priority of the biblical account of salvation history, and so the truth and historicity of its description of God's dealings with the world. But, like many of the early Church Fathers, he was also concerned to demonstrate the eternal meaning, the lasting relevance, of the biblical narrative, and a broadly Platonic understanding of the nature of knowledge as constituted above all by eternal ideas in the mind of God was useful to this end, though he was never self-consciously a Platonist in any accurate, technical sense.

Maurice's overwhelming conviction was that the ground of religious truth lay in the doctrine of creation. One of his favourite biblical books was the Gospel of John (this was a very characteristic enthusiasm of late nineteenth-century Anglican theologians), and it says there of the Word of God, in the opening chapter, 'All things were made through him, and without him was not anything made that was made.' (John 1.3) Maurice took that statement quite literally. All that is, is made by God. He followed the ancient, Augustinian tradition of seeing evil as a *privatio boni*, an absence of good. Therefore what is certain above all else is that the very ground of our being as human beings is our createdness. A phrase that recurs in his work is one taken from Coleridge – 'man as man'. This is not a crude apology for Victorian male chauvinism, but Maurice's way of saying 'human being as it really is, in the eyes of God'. As the Christian God is a God of love, humanity's creation is marked by a deep longing for union with God. Sin, conversely, for Maurice is not so much a *fundamental* flaw in human being – though he did accept the traditional concept of original sin – as a consequence of rebellion against God's will for us, an obstinate refusal to recognize and accept his desire for union with us. That is why Maurice characteristically talked of sin as separation from God.

But there was a further dimension to this argument that took him well beyond what many of his contemporaries were prepared to say. The divinely-implanted desire for union with God also implied a desire for communion with our fellow human beings. Separation, isolation, extreme individualism and selfishness were social sins. Human society for Maurice rested on God's will, and the fulfilment of that will would mean the creation on earth of a just and peaceable society. That is why the image of Kingdom recurs again and again in Maurice's writing. He was convinced that the Kingdom of God was an already existing fact, to be discerned underneath the chaos and imperfection of real human relations, as well as a future state towards which we should aim. Human beings were called to make real in their own lives the divine society, or Kingdom, that Christ had proclaimed in his ministry and teaching. Christian theology was therefore a social theology, and its message, far from being confined to some narrow compartment of our lives we might label 'private spirituality', was one for the whole of society.

It is true that Maurice did tend to use a rather simplified, schematic language for describing the divine origins of the world. He spoke constantly of a 'divine order', and found that order represented particularly in three levels of social identity – family, Church and nation.[4] At times it seems almost as if he reduces human history to the interaction of these absolute but abstract concepts. The Platonism, such as it is, is there in this very tendency to discern an underlying pattern in the varied matter of human history. And yet it would be quite wrong to think that what he does is to absolutize and justify existing social relations. The 'divine order' for him, like the concept of Christ's Kingdom, was a dynamic notion, which was never perfectly realized in any existing set of conditions, but represented as much as anything an ideal which Christians were called to discover and to embody in their lives. Once we have grasped that, for Maurice, Christian discipleship is at once deeply personal and yet also socially responsible, we can see that the 'divine order' is actually a call for social transformation.

The socializing of Christianity and the Christianizing of socialism

This takes us on to the next vital phase in Maurice's life. For all the lasting impact of *The Kingdom of Christ*, it is perhaps for his role in the formation of Christian Socialism above all that Maurice is remembered today. By 1848, the 'Year of Revolutions', Maurice was Chaplain of Lincoln's Inn and Professor of Theology at King's College, London. In that year, revolution in France stimulated the re-emergence in Britain of the radical democratic movement known today as 'Chartism'. The supporters of the Charter advocated things that have become familiar enough today – the secret ballot, universal suffrage, parliaments of fixed duration (i.e. regular elections). But in their day, these went far beyond what most of the middle classes wanted. With the capital cities of Europe in upheaval, to many in England the Chartist revival looked like a popular revolution in the making. A massive demonstration on Kennington Common, to be followed by a march to Parliament, was planned to take place on 10 April.

Maurice, with his friends Charles Kingsley and John Ludlow, was no less alarmed than his contemporaries. But they were convinced that the Church shared responsibility for the deterioration in social relations that in turn fomented popular unrest. By its individualistic emphasis on personal salvation, with a theology of rewards and punishments, Maurice thought that the Church of England had abandoned its vocation to embrace and transform the whole nation. It had ignored the duties of the rich in preaching the duties of the poor. Thus Chartism concentrated Maurice's despair at the failure of the Church to reach out to the labouring classes. The meeting on Kennington Common in fact proved a desperate anti-climax. Rain thinned the determination of the crowd, who were skilfully steered away from marching on Parliament. Chartism now began to fizzle out. But the temporary panic it had engendered left its mark on Maurice. With his friends, he started various ventures attempting to grapple with social problems – schools, a series of tracts, a newspaper, a series of co-operative businesses, and a Working Men's College. Of these only the last was to prove an enduring legacy of Maurice's Christian Socialism. It survives even today, as one of the oldest adult educational institutions in Europe.

Christian Socialism as Maurice conceived it had little to do with theoretical socialism, with Marx and the redistribution of property. Indeed politically Maurice was of a piece with many Liberal churchmen and politicians of his day – socially conservative, suspicious of democracy, but equally committed to resisting tyranny, and to defending moral and religious freedom. Rather, Christian Socialism for Maurice was simply another dimension of his concern for the Church. It arose out of his ecclesiology. It was an attempt to make the national vocation of the Church of England just that – a faith that would seek to renew and transform all classes, and all people. Maurice had an ingrained suspicion of religious elitism. He wanted to bring Christ to the poor as well as the rich, to Christianize the 'unchristian Socialists' and socialize the 'unsocial Christians'.[5] In some ways this was a mid-nineteenth century 'preferential option for the poor'. But it was to prove surprisingly tenacious. Almost unintentionally, given his own reservations about democracy and State-sponsored action, Maurice had provided theological inspiration for what was to become an enduring legacy of Anglican social thought. Later generations would take his 'Christian Socialism', with its appeal to the Church to live out in its own corporate life the principles of justice and fellowship that he saw as central to Jesus's teaching, and make of it something much more politically daring than Maurice himself ever imagined. His 'Kingdom' emphasis became in time a 'Kingdom theology'.

Heaven and hell

Christian Socialism was undoubtedly controversial, and it made Maurice's position at King's somewhat unstable. But by the time he founded the Working Men's College in 1854, he had already become embroiled in another, even more damaging controversy. In 1853 he had been forced to resign from his professorial chair at King's College, London, for appearing to doubt the doctrine of eternal punishment. In his *Theological Essays*, published in that year, he had denied that the New Testament word *aionios*, or 'everlasting', could mean the indefinite stretching out of periods of time. The punishment of the wicked could not be conceived as temporal punishment prolonged indefinitely. The infinite, in other words, could not be measured under the guise of finite concepts of time. Nor could heaven and hell be considered exclusively in terms of future states. Drawing on John 17.3 ('this *is* eternal life, that they may know you, the only true God, and Jesus Christ whom you have sent'), Maurice argued that the eternal life of the believer began in present faith, and in the knowledge of God. And he went further, when pressed. The notion of a God who willingly inflicted unending punishment was difficult to square with the loving God of the Gospels. Yet Maurice was not a universalist as such – that is, one who believed in the eventual salvation of all people, irrespective of their belief or moral actions. Eternal torment there might be, but it would be the consequence of a deliberate turning away from God, a wilful rejection of the source of all that was good and true, rather than the consequence of God's agency.

Interpretation of heaven and hell remains a controversial subject in Christian theology even today. When the Church of England's Doctrine Commission published *The Mystery of Salvation* some years ago, its outlining of a theory of hell in many ways similar to that of Maurice provoked criticism from a few quarters, though the main lines of

Maurice's view doubtless will not look particularly shocking to most readers now.[6] In Maurice's day, however, all sorts of dire implications were read into his eschatology. He was thought to be undermining the moral authority of the churches, challenging their ability to threaten with eternal punishment those who sinned and were unrepentant. The notion of religion as a system of rewards and punishments, which Maurice so severely attacked, was thought by many to be a vital prop of social order. Furthermore, wasn't Maurice apparently undermining the exclusiveness of salvation in Christ? Suspicion that this was the case might have been deepened by his remarkable lectures on *The Religions of the World* (1847), in which he had made an early and influential case for considering the great non-Christian faiths as carriers of truth and light. All this was too much for the governing Council of King's College.

Father of all

The effect of the controversy was to mark Maurice's reputation in the eyes of many church people, particularly Evangelicals and Anglo-Catholics. He was tarnished – unfairly, it has to be said – with the brush of heterodoxy, and when other storms broke over theological liberalism in the 1860s, Maurice was all too often simply put in the same category as people much more radical than he was. In fact, he was not just High Church in his view of the Church and the sacraments. He was also orthodox in his understanding of doctrine, and indeed quite conservative in his use of the Bible. He accepted the conclusions of the new science of evolutionary biology with ease (as did that other great Victorian theologian, John Henry Newman), but did not think it fundamentally contradicted the central truths of the Bible. Though he reinterpreted Christian doctrine in the light of contemporary concerns, he did not dilute it.

His novelty lay, rather, in his ability to look at the explanations theologians offered for Christian doctrine in a fresh light, and to take what were often long-buried insights and present them in a new way. He did this even with the central doctrines of the Christian faith about God. In his *Theological Essays* he put forward an argument for considering sociality as the very heart of the Christian understanding of the Trinity. The three-in-one was a community of persons, and relationship and mutual dependence was structured into the way the world was through God's making of it. As if to emphasize this, Maurice also stressed the

Fatherhood of God, seeing God as a loving Father of all, who was intimately bound up with, and concerned with, the lives of human beings, as a father with his children. Some would see this as a renewed stress on divine immanence – on the indwelling character of God in the created world. But it did not detract from Maurice's very strong sense of God's transcendence: the dependence of the world on God indicated that God was indeed the source of all, and beyond and above all. He was a loving Father who had made himself known to his people in Jesus Christ.

This conviction lay at the heart of the last great controversy of Maurice's life. In 1859 Henry Mansel, an Anglican theologian, delivered a series of lectures at Oxford entitled 'The Limits of Religious Thought Examined'. They were witty, sharp, clear rebuttals of contemporary scepticism, which defended Christian orthodoxy by turning the methods of the sceptical philosophers on their own profession of disbelief. Mansel, drawing on the philosophy of Immanuel Kant, in a sense agreed with the sceptics that religious truth was not accessible to critical reason, and that it was therefore meaningless to talk as if one could really 'know' God. Instead, one could only believe what had been proclaimed as true. If Mansel's goal was to uphold Christian orthodoxy, there were plenty of people who thought this was a peculiar way of doing so. Maurice was one of them. He was incensed by Mansel's apparently wilful ignoring of the intimacy of the Biblical language, and in a series of lectures and sermons, published as *What is Revelation?* (1859), he sought to stress both the transcendence of God and the fact that God has made himself known to us in such a way that we can say we know God as he is in himself.

Christ as Word and work

The lynchpin of Maurice's argument was, however, not so much the doctrine of revelation itself, as the doctrine of the Incarnation. The whole point of this, Maurice was saying in effect, was that the unknowable God had made himself known in a human person. A fully Trinitarian belief recognized that the intimacy the first disciples had known in their relationship with Jesus Christ was secured for all the followers of Christ in the life of the Spirit. Through faith, then, Christians are brought into a relationship with a real person, Jesus Christ, a person with whom it is possible to have a relationship in a sense comparable to that of other human relationships. Indeed, for Maurice the Incarnation was the focal point of Christian doctrine, because through it the eternal being of God was present in history, and all history, and all human society, therefore has its point of origin and its ultimate justification in the Incarnation of the Word. Again and again, though not in any systematic way, Maurice emphasized the doctrine of the Incarnation as the ultimate key to understanding human history – history, as it were, flowed towards and away from the Incarnation as the central axis (mixing metaphors) around which it turned.

This was also the basis of Maurice's somewhat less distinct attempt to reinterpret the doctrine of the Atonement. Just as he thought popular, debased Evangelical doctrine had tended to oversimplify the idea of future life and judgement, and turn it into something like a system of rewards and punishments that would appeal crudely to self-interest ('pie in the sky after you die'), so he also thought that the popular theology of penal substitutionary atonement had forced apart the doctrine of God and the doctrine of the Incarnation. If God was seen as a vengeful God, willing to inflict a penalty on his creation that could be averted only by the Son's substitution of himself for guilty humanity, then it seemed as if the loving Father of all was actually nothing more than a cruel tyrant. Not only did that seem morally questionable, but it also made it difficult to make sense of the intimate, apparently affectionate relationship with the Father we see Jesus articulating in the Gospels. Now Maurice did not swing decisively towards the ancient alternative to substitutionary theory, namely exemplarism – the idea that Jesus saves us through providing an example of willing, loving forbearance for us to imitate. Instead, in his *Theological Essays* and in his *Doctrine of Sacrifice* (1854), he sought to interpret the whole history of Israel, Jesus's mission on earth, and human destiny itself, as sacrificial – not in the sense of vicarious suffering, but in the (to Maurice) deeper sense of offering. The whole of the created order was in effect a continual offering to God, from God himself. Jesus was the one who demonstrated this inner reality, and supremely effected it in his offering of himself to death. Once again, in Jesus we find the focal point of human history, the disclosure of what is really and fundamentally true of human beings. There was thus no gulf between the will of the Father and the will of the Son: they were united in will, and thus Maurice could speak truly of the 'at-one-ment' of the Son and the Father. It is evident that here, just as in his view of eternal life, Maurice was concerned to remove the impression that God's motives could be read in the light of baser human values – in this instance, the desire for revenge. Instead, Maurice's reinterpretation of the Atonement both sustained the absolute and unconditioned agency of God, and threw the onus for human failure onto the all-too-common human tendency to deny God's will for us.

Death and reputation

Though he continued to write up until the year of his death, in many ways Maurice's most creative work had already been done by the early 1860s. In his circle of friends and admirers, he was still regarded with deep affection, indeed almost with reverence. A shy, hyper-sensitive and sometimes prickly man, at the same time he had, by all accounts, a breadth of sympathy that was deeply engaging. Yet outside his immediate circle of admirers, he was still regarded with some suspicion: the legacy of the controversies of the 1850s and early 1860s had not quite disappeared. His work was read with appreciation by a growing number of Anglicans and Dissenters, but it was not until his son's biography of him appeared in 1884 that Maurice's reputation began to rise substantially again. The *Life and Letters* presented a much more intimate, searching portrait of the man than had ever been evident from his published work, and it remains a vital source for understanding Maurice.

In time, the growing reception of Maurice's work filtered out what was often confusing and difficult from his work, and exposed the lasting elements of his thought. His social theology began to be adopted much more widely, shorn of its rather awkward appeal to national identity and to establishment. Maurice became a vital influence for a later generation of Christian Socialists, through whom eventually, in the twentieth century, inspiration for the development of the welfare state was to come. The growing ecumenical movement often looked to him as a figurehead too. Anglo-Catholics seeking to escape from what sometimes seemed a rigid traditionalism found in him inspiration for a 'mobile orthodoxy', a view of Christian faith that was fully consonant with church tradition and yet alert to the challenges of contemporary society.

At the heart of Maurice's legacy to the Church of England was a conviction that Christian disunity, whatever its sources, damaged Christian mission. Maurice was a committed Anglican, no less than in the conviction that the fullness of truth could not be encompassed in any one theological system, but in a comprehensive polity of the Church that could best hope to preserve the central convictions of Christians who disagreed with each other. This was not a faddish ecumenism. Maurice was seeking to confront a crisis in the moral and intellectual authority of the Christian faith which was replicated across Europe. Under concerted attack from political radicals, secularists, and revolutionaries, Christians were beginning to wake up to the fact that their own internal disagreements merely served to confirm the hostility of their critics.

Maurice's theology combined two contrasting insights: a biblical theology that was content to accept the Scriptures as a coherent living voice, and a metaphysical conviction of the universal nature of divine wisdom. At times it seemed as if he could hold these contrasting streams together only by sheer force of rhetoric. Yet his theology was both of its time and ahead of its time. It can help us to understand Anglicanism as it was in Maurice's day, but it can also sharpen up our understanding of the challenges and opportunities facing Anglicanism today.

Notes

1 F. Maurice, *Life and Letters of F. D. Maurice*, vol. I (1884), p. 153.

2 A. H. Ramsey, *The Gospel and the Catholic Church* (1936), p. 214.

3 See in particular T. Christensen, *The Divine Order: a Study of F. D. Maurice's Theology* (1973).

4 See below, pp. 103–5 (letter to A. J. Scott, 1839).

5 See below, p. 131.

6 'Hell is not eternal torment, but the final and irrevocable choosing of that which is opposed to God so completely and so absolutely that the only end is total non-being.' The Doctrine Commission, *The Mystery of Salvation* (1995), p. 199.

Part 2

An F. D. Maurice Reader

A Note on the Texts

In making the following selection of texts, I have borne in mind three main aims. First, I have tried to present key passages from Maurice's best-known works, in order to give my readers an insight into particularly important and distinctive aspects of his theology. Thus, there are substantial passages from *The Kingdom of Christ*, the *Theological Essays*, the *Doctrine of Sacrifice*, and *What is Revelation?*, as well as from some of the shorter pamphlets that usually touched directly on particular church controversies – indeed most of one of Maurice's best-known pamphlets, *Reasons for not Joining a Party in the Church*, is reproduced below. Second, I have generally avoided using very short extracts, in the belief that readers need also to have some insight into the way in which Maurice tended to develop an argument. Third, however, I have also wanted wherever possible to present texts that are generally comprehensible, or at least do not need a dense undergrowth of scholarly footnotes in order to clarify what they mean. For the last reason in particular, I have drawn quite freely on letters published posthumously, in his son Frederick's *Life and Letters of F. D. Maurice* (1884). The result is a rather eclectic mix of texts, organized in a thematic progression through Maurice's theology, but following a logical rather than strictly chronological organization within each chapter. Necessarily, this is all very selective indeed, and I cannot hope to give much more than a taste of Maurice's extraordinarily extensive body of work. Much has been omitted, including his thought on education and on non-Christian religions, since my goal has been to concentrate on his identity as an *Anglican* theologian.

Texts are reproduced exactly as they are found in the originals, with no alteration of spelling or punctuation, and italics and capitals retained too. Occasionally spelling is – to a modern reader – eccentric. Maurice may have been influenced somewhat by his brother-in-law Julius Hare's deliberate attempt to rationalize English spelling along phonetic lines, and of course in any case even by the mid-nineteenth century English orthography was by no means fully standardized. I have tried to keep references to a minimum, and have supplied them only in order to clarify what would otherwise remain obscure for the reader. One particular feature is worth noting, however. Maurice quoted freely from Scripture throughout his work, but evidently did not always check the accuracy of his quotations, and presumably relied on his memory of them. As a result, sometimes biblical quotations appear almost as paraphrases, and at other times they are woven seamlessly into Maurice's prose. I have not by any means indicated all of these references, but again only those which seemed to me to merit particular highlighting.

Finally, some comments about Maurice's idiosyncratic language may be in order here. The modern reader is likely to find Maurice's style a little more formal, rhetorical and elongated than is common today. On the whole I have chosen texts that are accessible, and anyone accustomed to reading Victorian novelists such as Dickens or Trollope will have no difficulty here. There is, however, an additional complication. Some words definitely had a resonance in Maurice's hands that was not usual in other writers. It would require a substantial essay on its own to identify all of the relevant terms, and explain them accordingly; in general it is easy to spot them. But a few words here may help to steer the reader towards a comprehension of Maurice's general sense. In almost all cases, what we find in Maurice's hands is a tendency to concentrate at least two different layers of meaning in one word, combining a sense of action or contingency with the notion of an underlying metaphysical reality being brought to the surface. Words such as 'discover' and 'educate' for Maurice are sometimes used to signify both the change brought about in a believer's life by a particular event, and the communication of eternal truth from God. In his *Theological Essays*, for example, in a passage quoted below, Maurice comments on the relationship of the Old and New Testaments to the effect that 'In both He [God] is *discovering* Himself to men; in both He is piercing through the mists which conceal Him from them.'[1] [My italics] Here the participle 'discovering' evidently carries both passive and active senses simultaneously: one denotes a revelation from God of God's own being, whereas the other signifies human receptivity to revelation. Again, in another passage quoted below, from one of his sermons, he describes the impact of the Trinitarian conception of God on human history: 'This was the name which the Father who had been seeking men to worship Him in spirit and in truth, had been *educating* them to know.'[2] [My italics] Here again the participle 'educating' is used in a slightly different sense from everyday usage, and indicates a double process of revelation from God and human learning through religious experience. The question of a certain residual Platonism in Maurice's work, touched on in the Introduction, is relevant here. These and other terms suggest how hard Maurice struggled to articulate his sense of the way in which the material world is suffused (as it were, sacramentally) with the presence of God.

Notes

1 See below, p. 78.
2 See below, p. 69.

I

Early Life and Views

The texts in this chapter illustrate the development of Maurice's thought, through letters written to his mother and father, and later in life to his son, Frederick. He never wrote an autobiography, but the first two letters, written in 1866, evidently were a first attempt to do so.

My Dearest Fred,

You have often begged me to write down some recollections of the sixty years through which I have passed. A fear of not reporting them faithfully and of being egotistical has kept me from complying with your request. But I hope to be tolerably honest. There will be enough in what I say to mortify my vanity if I am. And what I say will possibly be of use in warning you of tendencies which you may have inherited, and in leading you to seek a more effectual way of counteracting them than mine has commonly been. Above all it must show you, if I can but state the facts as they rise before my mind, what an education God is giving every one of us.

I say *every one*; for you will see nothing strange or exceptional in my biography. It is thoroughly commonplace, without startling incidents or peculiar conflicts, or any results which set me above the level of any of my countrymen. I have longed (how often!) in my silly vanity that I could give myself credit for something rare or great. But there has been a continual disappointment of this ambition, till at last I have learnt in some small measure to praise God for teaching me that I am one of a race, that He has been guiding me wonderfully, striving mercifully with my stupidity and obstinacy, setting an object before me when I was most turning away from it, because this is His method with all of us; because each may be brought to know that it is His method far more perfectly than I have been brought to know it, through my experience.

My letter to you last week on the 'Ecce Homo'[1] will have prepared you for the prominence which I give to the fact that I am the son of a Unitarian minister. I have been ashamed of that origin, sometimes from mere, vulgar, brutal flunkeyism, sometimes from religious or ecclesiastical feelings. These I perceive now to have been only one degree less discreditable than the others; they almost cause me more shame as a greater rebellion against a divine mercy. For I now deliberately regard it as one of the greatest mercies of my life that I had this birth and the education which belonged to it.

As I told you the other day, it has determined the course of my thoughts and purposes to a degree that I never dreamed of till lately. My ends have been shaped for me, rough hew them how I would, and shape has been given to them by my father's function and this name 'Unitarian' more than by any other influences, though I have been exposed to many of the most different kind which have strangely affected and may appear to some to have entirely disturbed that primary one.

My father's Unitarianism was not of a fiercely dogmatic kind. But it made him intolerant of what he considered intolerance in Churchmen or Dissenters; pleased when either would work with him, sensitive to slights from them. I have inherited from him some haste of temper, and impatience of opposition to what he thought reasonable. I wish I had anything like his benevolence, generosity, and freedom from self-indulgence. As I grew up I became far too sensible of what seemed to me his narrowness, and of a certain incoherency in his mind; far too little sensible of his very noble qualities of heart. I have since come to the practical conviction that this insensibility was a sin against God, a refusal to recognise the operations of His Spirit. I held that thought while I was with my father, but it was not a firm belief in my mind which could withstand a certain pharisaical conceit that I knew more than he did, and that I was therefore in some sense better. Now I am very sure that if I had this knowledge it made my moral inferiority to him an additional reason for shame and repentance. My mother had a far clearer intellect than my father, a much more lively imagination, a capacity for interests in a number of subjects, and an intense individual sympathy. In spite of her fancy, which made her very miserable by filling her with the most unnecessary fears about all who were dear to her, she was in all her own trials, even in sudden emergencies, brave and collected, and she had an inward truthfulness and love of accuracy which I have seldom seen stronger in any one; it gave a sort of curious definiteness to her apprehensions when they were the least reasonable.

For many years after my birth she was entirely agreed with my father in his religious opinions. Great differences arose between them afterwards which had a serious effect on my life; as you will find if I should be able to continue my narrative. I had three sisters older than myself. Two years before I was born my parents lost a little boy in croup. My mother could never utter his name; in all our intercourse I do not think she ever alluded to him; though I always perceived a shudder when any of us or any child for whom she cared was said to have the complaint which carried him off. In her papers there are many references to the boy. I think I must owe part of the peculiar tenderness which she always showed me to my having come in a certain degree to supply his place, though she was such a mother to us all that the word peculiar is somewhat out of place.

I have spoken of my parents before I have said anything about the place or time of my birth; but these two are influences, though subordinate influences in our education. I had the honour of being born on the same day (August 29) with a great Englishman whom perhaps I have not always appreciated as much as I ought, though I trust I have always reverenced his sincerity and manliness, John Locke. The sea-coast of Suffolk (my father's house was within a mile of Lowestoft) in 1805 was exposed to reports of French invasions. These were less numerous after the battle of Trafalgar, and I have only a vague impression of once having listened to some talk about them as I lay in my crib one night. We heard more frequently of poor men in whom my father was interested as being pressed for naval service; shipwrecks, and experiments for the establishment of life-boats also interested him greatly, and were topics which were discussed before us. These and some recollections of bathing are the only conscious impressions which I received from the neighbourhood of the sea. I cannot suppose that any boy does not derive unawares many influences from it which mingle with all the other currents of his life. About the war which was occupying all Europe during the seven years that I passed in Suffolk I cannot remember having heard anything.

My father was a strong Whig, as well as Dissenter. He had associated with those who were persecuted by Mr Pitt's Government and were suspected of French sympathies. I never found afterwards that he distinguished accurately between the first French war and the one which was connected with the freedom of Spain, Germany, Europe. He became ultimately a member of the Peace Society, and I should fancy had a dislike to all fighting at this time. He was not likely therefore to tell me much of Lord Wellesley's victories. I remember being taught Southey's lines on the Battle of Blenheim. I took it more literally than my parents could have wished, and supposed that Caspar, being an old and wise man, had disposed of his grandchild's objections to the very wicked thing. Some debate between my father and a music-master about Napoleon's expedition to Russia is all that comes back to me about the foreign events of that memorable time. On the other hand I have vivid impressions respecting some domestic events which now are almost forgotten. Sir Francis Burdett was a great hero of my elder sisters.[2] His going to the Tower and the watchword of his supporters took hold of my fancy, and remain in a memory from which many worthier things have departed. I recollect too the evening on which we heard the news of Mr. Perceval's assassination, and how the question whether Bellingham was sane or mad was debated in our house. My father farmed some land and also had a number of pupils. He was very much interested about agriculture, and probably knew something about it as it was then pursued.

I ought to have derived many more country tastes than I did from his example and conversation; he might too have cultivated in me a faculty of observation which he certainly possessed, at least, in some directions. But I was singularly the 'No Eyes' of the story which was read to me out of 'Evenings at Home,'[3] and anything social or political took a hold of me such as no objects in nature, beautiful or useful, had. My sister Emma said to me, when we were both grown up, that the scent of some violets which we gathered together as children at Normanstone had never passed out of her soul. How I envied her the freshness and freedom of heart which that experience implied!

Among my father's pupils there was one who became one of my kindest friends in after years. There are few men to whom I owe more than Alfred Hardcastle. He was attached to a cousin of mine, Anne Hurry. She was the daughter of my mother's eldest brother, and after her mother's death, when she was eleven years old she came to live in our house. My mother regarded her as a daughter; she must have been very attractive and clever. To me she was exceedingly kind, and took much pains both to amuse and instruct me. She had a younger brother Edmund, who also spent most of his time with us; and an elder, William, who was a man of unusual accomplishments; you must have seen him in his latter days after his return from India. His conversation in his best days was full of variety and interest. It gave me my first sense of what would be called in our days European culture.

His sister, who had many of his gifts, rather influenced me in another way. Besides her liveliness and wit there was a mystery about her attachment, which was broken off and then renewed, that linked itself with my feelings and impressions as a boy, and has never lost its connections with my manhood.

Thackeray says that every house has its 'skeleton.' If I may judge of others from ours, which had nothing the least to distinguish it, I should think every English house might have its heroines of flesh and blood, and might contain records of nobleness and constancy mixed with abundance of errors and contradictions, such as only those novelists can appreciate who believe (as I am satisfied Mr. Thackeray did) that God's creations are better than theirs, that facts are more precious than fictions.

From fictions of all kinds, modern or romantic, I was carefully guarded. Miss Edgeworth's 'Parents' Assistant' was the only storybook, I think, which ever came into my hands as a child; afterwards I was allowed her 'Moral and Popular Tales.' I have never approved or imitated this discipline. I have sometimes murmured against its effects upon myself, but I do not now regret it. I had the same temptations to speak falsely and act falsely as other children. I daresay I yielded to them as often. But I do think there was in me a love of truth for its own sake which has kept alive in me ever since. I do not know that the abstinence from fairy tales contributed to it. I am sure my mother's own sincerity cultivated it much more; and if my father had any hope of making me businesslike and scientific, he certainly failed. But I cannot be sure that, along with some dryness and poverty of fancy, I did not gain in this way a certain craving for realities which has been exceedingly necessary to me since I have begun to deal with abstractions of the intellect.

In 1812 we left Suffolk. My mother suffered from asthma. My sister Emma seemed to be in an atrophy. An aunt of mine, to whom my mother was much attached, was suffering from a spinal complaint at Clifton. She urged our coming there for the sake of the climate, and that Emma might be under the care of a medical man in whom she had great confidence. Emma's illness increased. She was attacked with water on the brain. But, to the wonder of all, she recovered and lasted till twenty-three, to be a blessing to every member of her family and to many beyond it.

In the year 1814 we removed to Frenchay, about four miles from Bristol, where I spent the next nine years of my life till I went to Cambridge.

Ever your affectionate father.

Life, I, pp. 12–18

[My dear Fred,]

When we left Suffolk a very excellent person, Miss Parker, was residing with us as governess to me and to my sisters Emma and Priscilla; the latter was three years old. Being very much attached to my mother she consented to go with us into Gloucestershire. She was, so far as I can judge from my early recollections, a very good teacher. That she was a wise and admirable woman I can have no doubt. My mother had taught me to read. Esther Parker, at her request and my father's, gave me very useful books to read, which I ought to have profited by much more than I did. I remember them now with a mixture of shame and amusement. 'Galton's Birds' and the 'Book of Trades' were conspicuous among them. The first I believe is as good a book as any on the subject till Bishop Stanley's appeared.[4] But I never knew the note of a single bird, nor watched the habits of any one. My book information, therefore, if such it was, speedily faded away. With so little care for natural history, I ought to have sympathised with the Trades. But the records of their wonders also fell quite dead upon my mind. It was not the fault of the books or of my teachers, nor even of the selection of subjects. There are many to whom either or both of these would have been interesting, in whom they would have awakened thoughts and activities which the common teaching of schools do not awaken. I am sure it was no superiority in my case, but a defect both of attention and sympathy, which has caused me much sorrow since, that made me irresponsive to such instruction. I do not recollect that I rebelled particularly against it. My passions, which were violent enough at times, were not excited by a dislike of particular studies or a preference for others. I had no great taste for reading of any kind; that which I delighted in most was anything dramatic. I was not indulged in this preference, but one or two stories of Miss Edgeworth, her 'Eton Montem' especially, had a very great charm for me. At a somewhat later time I began to care about history, but it was always such history as I could connect with the events which I heard of as passing in our time, or with some party feeling that had been awakened in me. My father being a Dissenter, I took great interest in a heavy and undoubtedly a somewhat narrow book, 'Neal's History of the Puritans.'[5] I owe much to the direction which this book gave to my thoughts; much even of the forms which my belief took when I became an Episcopalian.

My mind had thus received an early theological complexion, and my father greatly desired that I should be a minister among the Unitarians like himself. I took it for granted that I was to be so; he was not, of course, unwise enough to put a child upon the study of controversies. I was only recommended to read the Bible regularly, and many discussions about it went on in my presence. My Bible reading was a task which I performed every morning; I did not consider it on the whole an unpleasant task, but was rather proud when I had completed the proper number of chapters. There was something of formality about the old Unitarian conceptions of the Bible. My father believed in it more strongly and passionately than most of his sect, and was an enthusiastic champion of the Bible Society. But he encouraged a kind of criticism on it, which, though far short of that which has prevailed since, would shock many religious people now more than it did then. For the timidity about the contents and authority of the Bible has increased as it has become more exalted into an object of worship. To this exaltation the Bible Society on the one hand, and the Unitarian desire to separate it from the creeds on the other, have perhaps equally contributed.

But there came a great change over the spirit of our household. My cousin Anne Hurry had been particularly strong in Unitarian opinions; she had pursued them, I should suppose, more logically and consistently than my father, and had arrived at bolder conclusions. She became intimate with a very superior woman, who had been born a Quaker, and who now was a Moravian.[6] By this lady she was aroused to feel the need of a personal deliverer, such as her old system did not tell her of. The long illness and death of her brother Edmund, which took place in our house, deepened all her impressions. She had broken off the engagement with Mr. Hardcastle because they differed in their religious opinions. It was renewed, and they were married. My eldest sister went to visit her, and afterwards a clergyman in Sussex, whose wife was a relation of ours. She returned utterly dissatisfied with my father's opinions. My third sister, Anne, a very earnest, solitary thinker, who had long been studying such books as Law's 'Serious Call,'[7] sympathised with her, though their habits of mind were very unlike. My second sister, who was staying with her cousin when she died in her first confinement, arrived more slowly at the same impatience of Unitarianism. At first they were strongly influenced by Wesley's teaching. Gradually they all, for awhile, became strong Calvinists; the form of belief which was most offensive to Unitarians and to my father. It was still more grievous to him that they seemed to cut themselves off entirely from their childhood by undergoing a second baptism, and being connected with a Society of Baptist Dissenters. Very gradually my mother entered into their views. When her youngest child was born, many years after the others, she would not consent that there should be any baptism till it should be of age to determine for itself.

These events in my family influenced me powerfully; but not in the way which either of my parents or my sisters would have desired, nor in a way to which I can look back, so far as my then temper of mind was concerned, with the least complacency.

These years were to me years of moral confusion and contradiction. I had none of the freedom . . . [The manuscript from which this letter was copied to the *Life* ended here]

Life, I, pp. 18–21

To his mother, 9 December 1833.

My dearest mother,

Though I have felt grieved each day at reflecting on my delay in writing to you, I do not regret that I did not send my first thoughts, which I put down about a month ago; for as often, too often, is the case with mine, they are expressed in rather a complex manner, and might not have given you comfort. I now long and pray to be able to speak as simply as I ought to speak when I know that what I say is true.

My text is this, 'Know ye not that Jesus Christ is in you?'[8] The question is often put in such a way as to distress poor humble persons very much. But nothing was further from the Apostle's thoughts. To give a proud professor a notion that he had attained anything in having the Lord of Life near to him, to give the desponding spirit a gloomy sense of his distance from such a privilege, that was no part of Paul's commission or his practice. To prove it, see what he says, not to a faithful Christian or an unfaithful one, not to a church at all, 'For in Him we live and move and have our being.'[9] This is spoken to the ignorant, idolatrous inhabitants of Athens. What, then, do I assert? Is there no difference between the believer and the unbeliever? Yes, the greatest difference. But the difference is not about the *fact*, but precisely in the belief of the *fact*. God tells us, 'In Him,' that is in Christ, 'I have created all things, whether they be in heaven or on earth. Christ is the Head of *every* man.'[10] Some men believe this; some men disbelieve it. Those men who disbelieve it walk 'after the flesh.'[11] They do not believe they are joined to an Almighty Lord of life, – One who is mightier than the world, the flesh, the devil, – One who is nearer to them than their own flesh. They do not believe this, and therefore they do not act upon this belief. They do not think they are joined to Christ; and therefore they do not *pray*, that is, ask Christ to fill, animate, and inspire and sanctify them. They believe, for this is all they *see*, that they are surrounded by a *flesh* which shuts them in, that they are surrounded by innumerable objects of sense. Their hearts are wedded in the strictest sense of the word to sense, and they do not wish to be divorced. But though tens of hundreds and thousands of men live after the flesh, yea, though every man in the world were so living, we are forbidden by Christian truth and the Catholic Church to call this the real *state* of any man. On the contrary, the phrases which Christ and His Apostles use to describe such a condition are such as these: 'They believe a *lie*. They make a *lie*. They will not believe the *truth*.' The truth is that every man is in Christ; the condemnation of every man is, that he will not own the truth; he will not *act* as if this were *true*, he will not believe that which is the truth, that, except he were joined to Christ, he could not think, breathe, live a single hour. This is the monstrous lie which the devil palms upon poor sinners. 'You are something apart from Christ. You have a separate, independent existence.' See how this works. Separate from Christ, I can bear no fruit to God. Separate from Christ, I am separate from every one of my brethren. Then at once follows disobedience to God's two commands, 'Thou shalt love the Lord thy God; Thou shalt love thy neighbour as thyself.'[12] God commands *every* man to do this; but to command me, in myself, to love Him and love my neighbour is to command me an impossibility, to mock me with a precept which experience and reason and Scripture tell me cannot be performed.

Now, my dearest mother, you wish and long to believe yourself in Christ; but you are afraid to do so, because you think there is some experience that you are in Him necessary to warrant that belief. Now if any man, or an angel from heaven, preach this doctrine to you, I say, let his doctrine be accursed. You have this warrant for believing yourself in Christ, that you cannot do one living act, you cannot obey one of God's commandments, you cannot pray, you cannot hope, you cannot love, if you are not in Him. But God says, Pray, pray, hope, love; God bids me do that. He has constituted me to do, not something else, but just that. This condition I have made for myself; this state of independence, this fleshly Adam life is no state at all; it is a lie. In that I cannot please God. It is as impossible as that lying should please the God of Truth, as that enmity should please the God of Love. Wherefore we say to every man, 'In your flesh you cannot please God.' Wherefore we say to every man, 'Believe in the Lord Jesus, and you shall be saved.' Not, believe in a distant Christ, not, believe in a dead Christ; but, believe in the *Lord* Jesus Christ. Believe in Him as the Lord of your own spirit. Believe that your spirit is as much His servant as you have believed it the servant of the flesh. Believe Him to be mightier than the world around you, than your own flesh, than the evil spirit. Believe and live.

Now, who is the Lord of your spirit? He who agonised in Gethsemane, – He who died on Calvary, – the Lord of all love, – the

Lord who sacrificed Himself for love; this is the Lord of your spirit, ever near to you, ever present with you, with every one.

Does it grieve you because I say with every one, as if I put you on a level, as to hope, with the most vile and unbelieving? Oh, do not so pervert the words of comfort. The fact is, you desire earnestly that you could find one near you who loved you intensely, to whom you could tell your sorrows, your griefs, your sins; to whom you could tell everything in the assurance that He would sympathise with you, and that they, at present, do not feel this want. Then the same words spoken to you have as different a sound – as joy from grief – to them and to you. Yet I cannot disguise it, the words are the same. Ye are children of God; ye are members of Christ. Profligates, hard-hearted sinners, yea, hypocrites, this is your condemnation, that you are. It will be your misery to find that you were so, unless you will believe.

Now here is the warrant for *prayer*; here is the *possibility*, here is the *might* of prayer. Christ is in you, submit yourself to Him. Say, 'Lord, I submit.' Not now, but at every moment of your life; tell Him of whatever sins or sorrows are disturbing you; of *sins* no less than *sorrows*, of *sorrows* no less than *sins*. Of other people's sins no less than your own, of other people's sorrows no less than your own. Believe that He loves you and them. Ask that He will do His will in you, which is your blessedness. Ask that He will separate your spirit from the flesh and from surrounding objects by His spirit, in order that you may behold His love. Do not think you will ever have any righteousness or glory except His righteousness, for in perceiving this is your life, your happiness, your virtue, your glory. Ask Him to sanctify the whole body of which you are one member, that the whole body may see and delight in Him as its Head, and may not delight in themselves. For to delight in Him is righteousness, to delight in ourselves is sin. Lastly, ask Him more and more to shine through you, that others may see your good works and glorify your Father in heaven.[13] This He says He wishes, therefore, of course, He will do it for you. Tell me what you think of what I have said. May He bless it.

Life, I, pp. 154–7

To his father, 25 January 1834, on the eve of his ordination.

. . . If you ask me, my dear father, what feelings chiefly occupy me at this most important crisis of my life, I answer that they may be summed up in a desire for greater self-abasement and a more perfect and universal charity. I feel that the minister of the Gospel of Peace, the minister of a Church which is called Catholic and universal, is bound to have a much lower opinion of himself than I have practically and habitually of myself, and also to feel a much more perfect and unlimited love towards all and each than has yet ever been shown forth in me. When I speak of universal love, I do not mean any thing which is not perfectly consistent with national and family affection. I believe if we give up ourselves to God and renounce ourselves, He is sure to work these feelings in us, else why did He command us to have them? I long to have them far more strongly, in far more practical operation than I ever had. But I feel the duty of cultivating that universal love more incumbent upon me as a minister than upon others, because I think I am more directly shown the true foundation of it than others are. It is the natural feeling of all of us that charity is founded upon the uncertainty of the Truth. I believe it is founded upon the certainty of Truth. That God is Truth and Love also; that all men may know Him, that is, know Truth, and that He willeth all men to know Him; on this rock I build my charity. All error, all sin, in myself and in others is their misery; therefore I wish to hate it in myself and in them, and that they should hate it in me and in themselves, and trust with perfect confidence in God to deliver them and me out of it. Now this I feel is my imperfection that I do not love men's persons enough, and hate that which makes them unhappy enough; that I do not more labour to guide them into truth, and use the only means of doing so, kindness and love. This is my desire, this I am bound by my ordination vows to seek after; and, seeking, I trust that I shall find.

Life, I, pp. 158–9

To his eldest son, recounting events after his appointment as Chaplain of Guy's Hospital, undated [but text indicates 10 December 1870].

. . . That change in my circumstances did not bring me much into contact with London life. I was in an obscure corner, and my duties were such as would not have brought me acquainted with any who lived away from it. But Mr. Hugh Rose was at that time the Incumbent of the parish in which the hospital was situated, and was an intimate friend of Mr. Harrison, its treasurer; your uncle Julius [Hare], who was well acquainted with Mr. Rose, as they had both been Fellows of Trinity, though widely differing on the subject of which they both wrote,

German literature and theology, commended me to him. Partly through his influence, partly through that of Mr. Harrison's son, who had known me at Oxford, I obtained the chaplaincy.

I had been much impressed in my Bubbenhall curacy among labourers and farmers; I was still more impressed in the midst of this London population of sick men and women, with the language of our Catechism – that language which caused most offence to the Evangelical school. It seemed to me that except I could address all kinds of people as members of Christ and children of God, I could not address them at all. Their sin, it seemed to me, must mean a departure from that state; it must be their true state, that which Christ had claimed for them. I thought I had no Gospel for the sufferers in Guy's Hospital, if it was not that. – I was ignorant enough of their sufferings and sins, I knew that I was; my ignorance was unfathomable. If I might not say, God your Father knows it all, He is able and willing to raise you out of any depth into which you have fallen, I must despair. I could not think that they had ever resisted God's goodness as much as I had. I could not scold them, I could only speak to them of trust in One who could raise them. That became the principle of my preaching. I understood very little the way of making it intelligible to individuals, rich or poor, sick or well. But when preaching in the chapel or the ward, I found this language the only possible one. I felt therefore much sympathy with those who spoke of baptism as bearing witness of the state into which men are redeemed; I felt the worth of that direct appeal to the hearts and consciences of men which had distinguished the Evangelical preachers of the last century from the dry moralists, but I thought they had become weak, because they assumed sin, and not redemption, as the starting-point. The new form of churchmanship which was set forth in the Oxford Tracts had so far an attraction for me that it appeared to treat of a regeneration as dependent on the will of God and the death of Christ, not the individual faith of men. I did not care much for the other peculiarities of it, which were chiefly negative. It asserted that Presbyterians were not Churchmen, that Protestants and Romanists were equally departing from the standard of Anglican moderation. Such opinions had a certain influence, not a healthy one, on my mind, but they took no real hold of it. With that part which concerned baptism I dreamed for a while that I should have a real point of union. This dream was entirely scattered by Dr. Pusey's Tract on Baptism. Instead of affording me the least warrant for the kind of teaching which appeared to me alone Scriptural and practical, it made such teaching utterly impossible. The baptised child was holy for a moment after its baptism, in committing sin it lost its purity. That could only be recovered by acts of repentance and a system of ascetical discipline. I remember to this day the misery which this tract caused me as I read it in a walk to one of the London suburbs; I saw that I must be hopelessly and for ever estranged from this doctrine and from those who taught it, unless I abandoned all my hopes for myself and for the world.

Just about this time my eldest sister drew my attention to a movement in the Quaker body. The old Quakers had spoken of the divine Word as the light which lightens every man that cometh into the world. A younger body of them, who were in strong sympathy with the Evangelicals, declared that this doctrine interfered with reverence for the written word and with the doctrine of human depravity. Evidently the new party had much life in it and was conscious of a dryness and formality in the elder school. Reflecting much on this controversy and connecting it with what was passing in the English Church, it seemed to me that the old Quakers were affirming a most grand and important truth; but that it had become narrow and contradictory, because they had no ordinance which embodied it and made it universal; that we, on the other hand, forgetting their Quaker principles, or rather the words of St. John, necessarily made baptism a mere ceremony or a charm. The two being united expressed to me the reconciliation of the High Church Baptismal regeneration with the Evangelical demands for personal faith. Starting from this text, I wrote a series of tracts addressed to Quakers, but really concerning ourselves more than them. They formed the book called the 'Kingdom of Christ,' of which a second edition, much altered, appeared in 1841. In the second of these tracts I commented on Dr. Pusey's theory of baptism. Nothing I have written had so important an effect on my life. It set me in direct antagonism with his school, to which I had many attractions, and by some members of which my 'Subscription no Bondage' had been partially approved.

Soon the most advanced members of that school began to be exceedingly impatient of the articles for which they and I had pleaded. The younger men perceived that Dr. Pusey's baptismal doctrine was in spirit even more than in terms opposed to the maxims of the Reformation which had impressed themselves so deeply on our formulas. In his 90th Tract Dr. Newman undertook to show that there was a possible construction of the Articles which they might with a safe conscience recognise. His intention was, I am satisfied, honest, but to ordinary readers his interpretation appeared highly sophistical. Four Oxford tutors, one of them the present Archbishop of Canterbury, denounced it as fatal to all sincere subscription. This pamphlet called forth Dr. Hook, the present Dean of Chichester. He had sympathised much with the earlier tracts; he disliked the 90th; but he could not consent to abandon friends from whom he had learnt much. He said that the Oxford tutors compelled him to choose his party in the Church, and that he did choose that of their opponents. His book was the occasion of my 'Reasons for not Joining a Party in the Church.'[14]

Since my coming to Guy's Hospital I had become acquainted with Archdeacon Wilberforce, now the Bishop of Winchester. He was seeking, I believe, for a common ground between the two parties in the Church. He had a natural desire to see if any one else had found one. It was very unlikely that a man with his wide sympathies and knowledge of the world would do more than take a glimpse at the opinions of a solitary thinker and pass on. Every one who has been in temporary communication with him must be aware how great a power he has of receiving and reflecting impressions even from the least important persons.

Dr. Hook, who never sympathised with any of my opinions and knew little of me personally, yet wrote to me afterwards with characteristic generosity, that in this instance I had been right, and he had been wrong. The confession was far more honourable to him than to me, but no praise bestowed on me personally could have pleased me so much.

Thus you see that the principle with which I started became, almost in spite of me, the growing one of my life, that which every new circumstance made me more aware that I must live and die for, more aware also that it would separate me from those with whom I should most wish to act, and would give me not only the appearance of isolation and self-conceit, but often the reality of both. I knew also that I was in danger of attaching myself to a party which should inscribe 'No Party' on its flag. Many had fallen into that snare. I was as little likely as any one to escape it. The eminent man to whom I addressed my letters [Samuel Wilberforce] was one whom it was easy to follow as a leader in such an experiment as this. His especially genial qualities, the certainty that he would obtain and hold a reputation in English society, his personal kindness, were all powerful magnets. One of his most intimate friends had at that time a real regard for me, and a sympathy with some of my convictions.[15] I spoke so much of them, and looked up so much to them, that Sterling and others looked upon me as one of their fraternity.[16] Our common dread of the Liberals, the Evangelicals, and the High Church school might have bound me slavishly to their modes of thinking if God had not given me a nearer friend who understood me better than they understood me or than I understood myself. Your mother knew the secrets of true Churchmanship better than any of my male acquaintances, and oh, how much better than I did!

'If you only act on your conviction,' she once said to me, 'that Christ is in every one, what a much higher life you might live, how much better work you might do!' There was in that sentence the clearest divination of what I feel and know to be God's purpose in all His teachings and discipline which I have received, and of my failures.

I was sent into the world that I might persuade men to recognise Christ as the centre of their fellowship with each other, that so they might be united in their families, their countries, and as men, not in schools and factions; and through forgetfulness of this truth myself I have been continually separating myself from relations, letting go friendships, and sinking into an unprofitable solitude.

Your mother sought to save me from this vanity, making home more delightful than any other society could be, and yet giving me an interest in that, yet teaching me that the poorest man is Christ's brother and should be dear to us for His sake. She mourned over my want of sympathy with nature, and many deeper wants than that; yet she entered into all my thoughts and pursuits. She and your second mother have shown me how much a married man may be, if he will, educated by marriage in the kingdom of God, how much the true union of hearts may make party ties unnecessary to him. God's love has been at the root of their wedded lives; if it had been equally of mine there would not be so much shame mixed with joy and thankfulness in the recollection of what I have written and what I have been. But joy and thankfulness should and shall triumph over the shame. God blots out the sins and keeps alive all that is pure and good. I can bless Him that He has not suffered me to join a party in the Church in my youth, or manhood, or old age. I can believe on this tenth day of December, 1870, your mother's birth-day, that she is helping you, and your brother, and me, and teaching us more than if she were visible to us of our union with each other and with all in Christ.

Life, I, pp. 235–40

Notes

1 *Ecce Homo* (1865), by Sir John Seeley (1834–95), was a best-selling book retelling the life of Jesus as a religious reformer.

2 Sir Francis Burdett (1770–1844) was a Radical politician, briefly imprisoned in the Tower of London in 1810.

3 A reference to *Evenings at Home* (1794) by Anna Letitia Barbauld (1743–1825).

4 Edward Stanley (1779–1849) published a two-volume study of British birds in 1836.

5 Daniel Neal's *History of the Puritans* (1732–38) was a classic text for English Dissenters.

6 The Moravians were a small sect of Evangelical believers who had originated in a community of persecuted Protestants from Moravia established by the Pietist Count Nicholas von Zinzendorf on his lands in Saxony in the early eighteenth century; they profoundly influenced John Wesley.

7 *A Serious Call to a Devout and Holy Life* (1728), by William Law (1686–1761), was a popular manual of practical and devotional morality.

8 2 Corinthians 13.5.

9 Acts 17.28, where Paul is described as quoting the Cretan poet Epimenides's poem *Cretica*.

10 Apparently a paraphrase of 1 Corinthians 11.3, turned into a comment on Christ's universal headship.

11 A quotation either from Romans 8.1 or 2 Peter 2.10.

12 Apparently a paraphrase of Luke 10.27.

13 Maurice here draws freely on Matthew 5.16.

14 See below, pp. 113–21.

15 A reference to Richard Chevenix Trench (1807–86), at this time Archbishop of Dublin.

16 John Sterling (1806–44), famous for his friendship with Thomas Carlyle as well as with Maurice.

2

Faith, Fellowship and Theology

A selection of extracts from letters and published works here demonstrates Maurice's conviction that faith is based on a broad, living apprehension of God's goodness and creative power, and that all human systems of thought have a tendency to narrow this ground into a form of selfishness. The Bible, for Maurice, was a standing rebuke to this creaturely limitation. The theologian's task, for Maurice, was not to construct a great system of doctrine of his own, but to 'dig down' into the received wisdom of the Scriptures and the Church's tradition, and to unearth and reinterpret afresh the richness of Christian truth.

To Georgina Hare, 29 December 1847.

. . . I have just been reading a long and elaborate review of my 'Kingdom of Christ' in a German periodical. It is written by Sack, who is very courteous and complimentary, though he differs from me in nearly every point, and takes great pains to show how wrong I am.[1] He has taught me to see more clearly than I ever did what the ground of my difference with the Evangelicals, both of England and Germany, is. The latter, though so much wiser and more cultivated, still seem to make sin the ground of all theology, whereas it seems to me that the living and holy God is the ground of it, and sin the departure from the state of union with Him, into which He has brought us. I cannot believe the devil is in any sense king of this universe. I believe Christ is its king in all senses, and that the devil is tempting us every day and hour to deny Him, and think of himself as the king. It is with me a question of life and death which of these doctrines is true; I would that I might live and die to maintain that which has been revealed to me. I think that one who understood what I meant better than all the doctors, and only lamented that I acted so little up to my conviction, is now sharing my faith with me, strengthening me in it, and in the darkest hours giving me increased tokens and assurances of its truth.[2] I think that is no dream, nor yet that she is with you, teaching you and cheering you.

Life, I, pp. 450–1

On sin as a rejection of God's ordering of the world.

. . . Man is in society, each man is a distinct, living, responsible man. It would seem that this is a fact of our constitution; but we must understand that constitution in order to explain it . . . This is the very question, which, in different ways, this age is asking itself . . . Tell us then the secret, if you know it. If you cannot, we will tell you. We have been telling it to the children in our charity schools these many years past. We teach them out of the Catechism, that they are children of God, members of Christ, heirs of the kingdom of heaven. We expound to them what we believe to be that universal constitution for man as man. We believe that we are admitted by baptism into this constitution, and laid under an obligation of making it known to other men as intended also for them. We believe that a man not understanding this constitution, attempting to set up a separate individual life, does divest himself of his glory as a man, does not fulfil the duties of a man. We believe that the man, who, receiving the good news that there is this constitution, and renouncing and repenting of the selfish life he has led, living as if he were personally related to the head of the polity, rejoicing to think that he is so (because he is a man, and not because he is any particular man) does rise to a feeling of personal distinctness which he can never get in any other way, and which is so essential to his being, that all moral or spiritual cultivation without it is impossible.

SNB, pp. 44–6

Living faith is to be distinguished from religious convention.

To Daniel Macmillan, 28 June 1844.

. . . The one thought which possesses me most at this time and, I may say, always has possessed me, is that we have been dosing our people with religion when what they want is not this but the Living God, and that we are threatened now, not with the loss of religious feeling, so-called, or of religious notions, or of religious observances, but with Atheism. Everywhere I seem to perceive this peril. The battle within, the battle without is against this; the heart and the flesh of our countrymen is crying out for God. We give them a stone for bread, systems for realities; they despair of ever attaining what they need. The upper classes become, as may happen, sleekly devout for the sake of good order, avowedly believing that one must make the best of the world without God; the middle classes try what may be done by keeping themselves warm in dissent and agitation to kill the sense of hollowness; the poor, who must have realities of some kind, and understanding from their betters that all but houses and lands are abstractions, must make a grasp at them or destroy them. And the specific for all this evil is some evangelical discourse upon the Bible being the rule of faith, some High Church cry for tradition, some liberal theory of education. Surely we want to preach it in the ears of all men: It is not any of these things or all these things together you want, or that those want who speak of them. All are pointing towards a Living Being, to know whom is life, and all, so far as they are set up for any purpose but leading us into that knowledge, and so to fellowship with each other, are dead things which cannot profit.

Life, I, pp. 369–70

On justification through faith.

[If we] believe that the Christ, the King of man's spirit, having taken the flesh of man, willingly endured the death of that of which flesh is heir, and that His Father, by raising Him from the dead, declared that death and the grave and hell could not hold Him, because He was His righteous and well-beloved Son, we have that first and highest idea of Justification which St. Paul unfolds to us. God justifies the Man who perfectly trusted in Him; declares Him to have the only righteousness which He ever claimed, – the only one which it would not have been a sin and a fall for Him to claim, the righteousness of His Father, – the righteousness which was His so long as he would have none of His own, so long as He was content to give up Himself. '*He was put to death in the flesh, He was Justified in the Spirit*;'[3] this is the Apostle's language; this is his clear, noble, satisfactory distinction, which is reasserted in different forms throughout the New Testament. But St. Paul takes it for granted that this justification of the Son of God and the Son of man was his own justification, – his own, not because he was Saul of Tarsus, not because he was a Hebrew of the Hebrews, but because he was a man. All his zeal as an Apostle of the Gentiles, all his arguments against his own countrymen, have this ground and no other; the one would have worn out from contempt and persecution, the other would have fallen utterly to pieces, if he had not been assured that Christ's resurrection declared

Him to be the Son of man, the Head of man, and therefore that His justification was the justification of each man. He had not arrived at this discovery without tremendous personal struggles. He had felt far more deeply than Job did how much he was at war with the law of his being, the law which he was created to obey; he had felt far more deeply than Job that there was a righteousness near him and in him, in which his inner mind delighted. He had been sure that there must be a Redeemer to give the righteousness the victory over the evil, to deliver him out of the power to which he was sold, to satisfy the spirit in him which longed for good. He had thanked God through Jesus Christ his Lord. And now he felt that he was a righteous man; that he had the only righteousness which a man could have, – the righteousness of God, – the righteousness which is upon faith, – the righteousness which is not for Jew more than for Gentile, – which is for all alike.

TE, pp. 170–1

On the Bible as a check to human error.

To Charles Kingsley, 19 July 1844.

. . . With respect to the study of the Scriptures, my own great error has been that I have formed and abandoned so many plans, any one of which honestly pursued, might have led to good results. I fancy this is a prevalent temptation, though I have yielded to it and suffered from it more than any other of my acquaintance. As I would turn diseases to commodity, or, at least, as God is sometimes mercifully pleased to do this for us, I think I may say that all the deplorable waste of time which these changes have occasioned has brought with it this compensation, that I had been solemnly and inwardly impressed with the truth that the Bible, as a means of attaining to the knowledge of the living God, is precious beyond all expression or conception; but, when made a substitute for that knowledge, may become a great deadener to the human spirit than all other books. The method of the Bible itself, and the reasons of its being overlooked, I think, become more and more clear to us as we keep this consideration before us. If it be a human history containing a gradual discovery of God, which discovery awakens the very faculties and apprehensions which are to receive it, the treatment of it as a collection of notions either about the invisible world or our own duty must entirely mislead us in all our studies; and, whether we rate it high or low, whether we accept it as the one rule of faith, maintain its authority to be concurrent with that of Church traditions, or look upon it merely as a set of fragments containing the speculations of a certain nation about religious questions, the result will be much the same. In each case the end of the book will be lost, and therefore all the steps to that end will be confused and incomprehensible. But if once the teachers in our theological schools would have courage to proclaim theology to be the knowledge of God and not the teaching of a religion, I am satisfied that the scientific character of the Bible would be brought out as conspicuously as its practical character, one being seen to be involved in the other. Then it would not be necessary to assert for theology its place as the *scientia scientiarum* [science of sciences], or to bid others fall into their places in connection with it and subordination to it; far less would it be necessary to be perpetually proclaiming Church authority in favour of such and such doctrines. The truths concerning God would be felt so essential to the elucidation of those concerning men and nature, the relation of one to the other would be so evident, there would be such a life infused into the portions of human knowledge, and such a beautiful order and unity in the whole of it, that the opposition to them would be recognised as proceeding just as much from prejudice and ignorance, sure to disappear whenever these came with moral causes to sustain them, as the opposition to gravitation or any of the most acknowledged physical or mathematical principles. I do not mean that this effect would follow suddenly, or that the actual impediments to the Gospel from human pride and wickedness would be less felt – I suppose they would be more felt – after it had followed. But we should then be obliged to acknowledge that much of the resistance to the most precious principles may actually proceed from a love to some others, or even to those same; we should not have such a din of voices crying out for this theory and that, and many forgetting God in their love for abstractions; we should not see so much violent straining and perverting of truth to serve a purpose; we should have much less idolatry of the Bible, and much more reverence for it. And the hard-working of our parishes, having been trained in such a school before they entered upon practical duty, would find a clearness in their minds, a readiness for occasions, a power of bringing their studies to bear upon life, instead of being obliged, as is now so much the case, either to shut their eyes against any new light or else to destroy and reconstruct their system each time that any is vouchsafed to them. But since our Universities afford us no teaching of this kind at present we must try to profit by the helps which we have. Our actual work is, I think, the best of these helps. It forces us, whether we will or no, out of the routine of sects and systems, and leads us to seek for something in Scripture which is altogether unlike them. And though I would strongly urge any one not to lose the idea of that method of which I have spoken, I would by no means recommend any one who was not working as a professed theologian in the schools to spend his time in contriving how he may adjust his own reading to it. The use of it to him will be far greater if he recollects that it exists when he is reading a single book or chapter or text, than if he determined doggedly to make out the traces of it from Genesis to Revelation. The subject of his studies, I should think, must be always best determined by the wants of his parish.

Life, I, pp. 372–4

Maurice describes the aim of his social theology as not to propound new theories, but to demonstrate the divine ground of all true society.

To John Malcolm Ludlow, 24 September 1852.

My Dear Friend,

You treated my anti-democratical heresies with great tenderness, of which I should not have been worthy, if I had really given myself credit for any antiquarian knowledge which I suspected you of wanting. I have little enough of that, as well as of that acquaintance with the present condition of legal, political, and economical science, which I have always envied you for. And that was nearly what I meant by calling myself a digger merely. If I had not been afraid of your mistaking me, I should have given myself the grand title of a theologian, and said that, leaving other spheres of thought and activity to those who were destined for them, and had been furnished with the gifts appropriate to them, I had taken my ground on that one study in which most people would say that I had a professional interest, but which most regard as hopelessly barren. But such a statement would have been misleading, unless I had impressed you with my own deep conviction that theology is not (as the schoolmen have represented it) the climax of all studies, the Corinthian capital of a magnificent edifice, composed of physics, politics, economics, and connecting them as parts of a great system with each other – but is the foundation upon which they all stand. And even that language would have left my meaning open to a very great, almost an entire, misunderstanding, unless I could exchange the name theology for the name God, and say that He Himself is the root from which all human life, and human society, and ultimately, through man, nature itself, are derived. I tried to express all in that one phrase that I was a digger, intending distinctly *this*, that I fear all economics, politics, physics, are in danger of becoming Atheistic: not when they are worst, but even when they are best; that Mill, Fourier, Humboldt, are more in danger of making a system which shall absolutely exclude God, and suffice without Him, than any less faithful and consistent thinkers – that, just so far as we are chiefly constructive, this danger becomes more imminent and tremendous, that the destructive analysis of the last century is not so alarming as the synthesis of our own.[4]

Therefore let people call me merely a philosopher, or merely anything else, or what they will, or what they will not; my business, because I am a theologian, and have no vocation except for theology, is not to build, but to dig, to show that economy and politics (I leave physics to dear Kingsley, who will in that region, and in every other, carry out my hints in a way I could never dream of, and which I admire with trembling, hope, and joy) must have a ground beneath themselves, that society is not to be made anew by arrangements of ours, but is to be regenerated by finding the law and ground of its order and harmony, the only secret of its existence, in God. This must seem to you an unpractical and unchristian method; to me it is the only one which makes action possible, and Christianity anything more than an artificial religion for the use of believers. I wish very earnestly to be understood on this point, because all my future course must be regulated on this principle, or on no principle at all. The Kingdom of Heaven is to me the great practical existing reality which is to renew the earth and make it a habitation for blessed spirits instead of for demons.

To preach the Gospel of that Kingdom, the fact that it is among us, and is not to be set up at all, is my calling and business. Because I have preached it so uncertainly – like one beating the air – I have had an easy, quiet life; far too much of the good opinion of my friends; merely a few lumps of not hard mud from those who, now and then, suspect that I have hold of something which might make me their mischievous enemy. But if ever I do any good work, and earn any of the hatred, which the godly in Christ Jesus receive, and have a right to, it must be in the way I have indicated, by proclaiming society and humanity to be divine realities, *as they stand*, not as they may become, and by calling upon the priests, kings, prophets of the world to answer for their sin in having made them unreal by separating them from the living and eternal God who has established them in Christ for His glory.

This is what I call digging, this is what I oppose to building. And the more I read the Epistle to the Corinthians, the more I am convinced that this was St. Paul's work, the one by which he hoped to undermine and to unite the members of the Apollos, Cephas, Pauline, and Christian (for those who said 'we are of Christ' were the worst canters and dividers of all) schools. Christ the actual foundation of the universe; not Christ a Messiah to those who received Him and shaped Him according to some notion of theirs; the head of a body, not the teacher of a religion, was the Christ of St. Paul. And such a Christ I desire to preach, and to live in, and die in. Only let us each work in the calling whereto God has called us, and ask Him to teach us what it is, and we shall understand one another and work together.

Life, II, pp. 136–8

Notes

1 The reference here is to Karl Heinrich Sack, 1789–1875, a German Reformed theologian who published books on the Church of England (1818) and the Church of Scotland (1844); I have been unable to trace the review in question, however.

2 A reference to Anna Barton, née Barton, Maurice's first wife, and mother of his two sons.

3 This appears to be a conflation of 1 Timothy 3.16 and 1 Peter 3.18.

4 J. S. Mill (1806–73), English philosopher; Charles Fourier (1772–1837), French social theorist; Wilhelm von Humboldt (1767–1835), Prussian political philosopher.

3

The Incarnation

Maurice did not write a substantial work on the Incarnation of Christ, but it is a constant preoccupation of his writing. The texts assembled here demonstrate how central it was to his interpretation of history, as well as to his understanding of Christian theology. In his sermon, 'Christ among the doctors', taken from What is Revelation? *(1859), he attempts to explain how the divinity of Christ did not cancel out or qualify his humanity, but rather was a perfect embodiment of humanity, even at the stage of his earthly life as child.*

On the Incarnation as the key to the history of Israel.

[The] expression 'word of God' is one of continual recurrence as well as of most solemn import in the books of the Old Testament. I could not find that, in its lowest sense, it ever meant less than a message from the invisible God to the mind and spirit of man. The assertion that God speaks to men by His word, and that men are capable of hearing that word, was the great testimony for the truth which was implied in heathen superstitions, the great testimony against these superstitions. Idolaters were not mistaken in thinking that they needed intercourse with that which was higher than themselves; they *were* mistaken in seeking, in the heaven above, or in the earth beneath, or in the water under the earth, for Him who was nearer to them than He was to all the things He had made, who was the Lord of their hearts and reins. The more you study the Law, the Psalms, and the Prophets, the more you meditate the earliest and simplest book of the Bible – that which tells of the Voice which spoke to Adam in the garden, of the Voice which called Abram to go forth whither he knew not – the more, I am persuaded, you will feel that this is the most characteristic peculiarity of these records, that which connects them with each other, that which has given them their power over mankind.

Nevertheless, the life of the men who were said to receive these communications was eminently practical and manly . . . While they kept their faith in the unseen Teacher, the firmament over their heads became a clear daily and nightly witness respecting Him and themselves . . . The Jew was taught that the Lord God was his King; that He broke the yoke of the Pharaoh and of the Pharaoh's gods; that He claimed the most abject slaves as His servants. The Israelite was brought under an order which had this foundation. In the strength of it, kings were to reign and decree judgment; they were to preserve the people from lapsing into the idolatry which would destroy their obedience and their freedom. They were to reign by the word of the Lord.

But what was this word of God which held men back who had fierce inclinations in their hearts, and who had swords to execute them in their hands? It could not be a statute; that had no such power. It could not be a set of moral maxims; they had no such power. It could not be a promise, or a threat, about the world that is, or the world to come; neither had such power. The Prophet, living amidst the signs of decay and ruin in his own polity, amidst the earthquakes which were shaking all nations, under the overwhelming power of empires that sought to put out the life of nations, began to attach another and deeper sense to the word of God, not incompatible with the older use, but involved in it; not a metaphor or allegory deduced from it, but a higher truth lying behind it. The Word of God came to him, spoke to him in the very depths of his heart. He spoke to it, sympathised with it. But dared he say *it* any longer? No, in some wonderful manner this Word must be a Friend, a Person; One who could work with him, reprove him, illuminate him. This Word must be the Teacher, the Friend, the King of Israel. The Word must one day prove Himself to be the Lord of the whole earth. Awful discovery! which makes him tremble, and yet which makes him bold; which sometimes draws forth from him the cry, '*Woe is me! for I am an unclean man, and I dwell among a people of unclean lips; for mine eyes have seen the King, the Lord of Hosts*;'[1] which again gives him all his hope both for himself and for his people. At every step of his own experience and of his nation's experience, new visions unfolded themselves out of this vision. It must be that all those various objects in nature which men were worshipping, that all the living order of nature in which those things were comprehended, proceeded from this living Word. It must be that all the races of men, all their polities, were under His guidance and government. It must be that all the light that had entered into any man's heart had come from Him. It must be that the darkness which was in any man's heart had come from rebellion against Him.

TGSJ, pp. 16–18

On the Incarnation as God's descent into all humanity.

[Why] must we think that this person [Jesus Christ] was more than *a* shrine of the Holiest? why should we speak of Him as *the* One? why should this name of 'the Only-Begotten' be bestowed upon Him? Again I say, Withhold it if your heart and conscience bid you do so. But do not deceive yourselves. The question is not any longer, whether there should be an Incarnation, whether God can manifest Himself in human flesh; but *what* the Incarnation should be, in what kind of person we are to expect such a manifestation, or whether He will diffuse His glory through many persons, never gathering it into one. With respect to the former question, the Church has always admitted, the Apostles eagerly asserted, that the demand which they made upon human faith was enormous. The glory of God revealing itself, not in a leader of armies, a philosopher, a poet, but in a carpenter, – could anything be more revolting? There was no shrinking from the shameful confession. It was put forward prominently; it was part of the Gospel which was preached to Jews, Greeks, Romans. And it was received as a Gospel, a message of good, not of ill, because the heart of man answered, 'We want to see, not some side of earthly power elevated till it becomes celestial; we want not to see the qualities which distinguish one man from another dressed out and expanded till they become utterly unlike anything which we can apprehend or attain to. We want to see absolute Goodness and Truth. We want to know whether they can bend to meet us. That which cannot do this is not what we mean by Goodness. It is not what we should call goodness in any man. That truth which belongs to a few and not to all is not what we mean by Truth. The truest man we know has a voice which commends itself to all, which reaches even the untrue, if it be but to frighten and incense him. The goodness which can stoop most, which becomes, in the largest sense, grace, – the truth which can speak to the inmost heart of the dullest human creature, is that which has for us the surest stamp of divinity.'

TE, pp. 92–3

In his sermon, 'Christ among the doctors', a reflection on Luke's story of the child Jesus surprising the teachers (here, 'doctors' or Rabbis) in the temple leads Maurice to explore the perfection of Christ's humanity as a child.

. . . [All] is suitable to the boy. He pronounces on nothing. He does not lay down the law upon this matter or that. The time may come when He shall go up into a mountain and open His lips, and speak as one having authority. But that time is not yet. He is not above the Scribes, but is sitting at their feet. He desires to know what they think about this commandment in the Law, about this sentence of David or Isaiah. At first, no doubt, the answers are all ready. They can tell that which one elder or another had written down or expressed orally to his disciples. They begin to give out the oracles, perhaps with an air of patronage or condescension, to the earnest youth. Why do the patronage and the condescension disappear? Why is the well-trained memory at fault? Why is there that look of puzzle and perplexity, almost of terror, on the countenance of those who are used to resolve all riddles, to silence all disputes? The question has gone beneath commentary and text both. The second-hand answer does not avail. What, for instance, could it profit to give the best exposition of the Commandments, if the Child with those deep, searching eyes said: 'He who spoke these commandments calls himself The Lord *thy* God. What is this *Thy*? Is He indeed the God of each of you? He speaks as if He were a deliverer out of bondage. Is that indeed so? Was He only a Deliverer of our fathers in the days of old, or is he that still, that now? The prophets always describe Him as the Living God – the God from generation to generation. What! Is He then actually with us as He was with them, speaking to us as He spoke to them? He is described as a Father pitying His children, putting away their sins from them, and yet as hating all iniquity. Is that so still? Does He actually seek to make men right?'

I have supposed, you see, questions which had no novelty or strangeness in them; questions which arose directly out of the language of the Holy Book. If these had been all, – if there had been none deeper than these – deeper than we can think of, – what must have been their effect? No Rabbi can have imputed captious doubt, premature disbelief, to the *speaker*. May not many a one have been led to suspect *himself* of doubt and disbelief?

. . . No doubt He showed as much willingness to submit to their catechism as He had shown eagerness to receive whatever they had to impart; a child, whichever task he was engaged in, – taught by elder men, doing what they required. And the answers, we may be sure, like the questions, would not be new or rare or far-fetched. They would be startling because they presented the words of holy men in their direct, full, original force; because they did not make veils for the sense, but drew away a veil which had concealed it; because the words came forth in them as if the men were there in whose hearts they had been as a burning fire; because the words were shown to be not theirs, but His who had spoken to them, and had declared His own purpose through them . . .

It was therefore, as the Evangelist expresses it, the *understanding* of this child which astonished the doctors. We can see what must have been the impression upon their minds. This boy entered into the very sense of the words which they had read and copied and committed to memory. They had never *understood* the words as spoken to themselves. They had drawn conclusions from the words, generalized notions from them. But their hearts had never come into contact with them . . .

. . . Although, therefore, one discovers nothing in the listening or questioning or answering of this Boy which interferes with that growth in wisdom and stature of which St Luke speaks, – with that gradual unfolding of the human life which was necessary to the manifestation of the Divine life, – there is *that* foreshadowing of after-years which we generally discern in an individual man when we are acquainted with the facts of his story, and which we should confidently expect in *the* Man, the Representative of the Race.

WR, pp. 24–8

Christ as the peacemaker.

In such a Person, then, that one new man in which Jewish and Gentile elements might both be reconciled, could be found. And surely only in such a One. If there were no such Being, no one of whom it could be said, He is the complete manifestation of God, He is the living centre of all human beings and of all human thoughts, I do not see what explanation we have of the history of the old world, or of its passage into the modern. But without Him I can as little understand how there is ever to be peace in that jarring world to which we belong. That the coming into it of the Son of Man was the sign that peace was meant for the earth and good will to men, the Angels' song proclaimed. That the coming of the Son of Man into it was not to bring peace, but rather a sword, that it was to make a man's foes those of his own house, He himself proclaimed. History has interpreted the paradox. Because He is the Prince of Peace, all the enemies of peace within the heart of man have been stirred up, all have found that they had a common interest in driving Him out of His proper kingdom. And this is not all. He does not come to make a solitude and call it peace; He does not come to destroy all that is distinctive in nations or in individuals, for the sake of producing a dead uniformity. He comes to arouse men, and all the thoughts and energies of men, out of sleep; not to put them into sleep. All that is strongest in man hears His voice and starts into life. Therefore the Jew becomes more intensely a Jew, and the Gentile more intensely a Gentile, before they consent both to receive their law from Him. And when they do receive it, though it crushes their pride, it justifies His Father's purpose in the destiny which He has fixed for them, in the education which He has given them . . .

. . . Where is this [history of human conflict] to end? We have tried all schemes. Persecutions, accommodations, indifference, all have had their turn; all have been practised under the most favourable circumstances, by persons resolute to make them succeed, and possessing all means and appliances for effecting their purpose. And still the question is heard through earth and rises to Heaven, Whence is Peace to come; – Peace from the strivings which are rending the heart of mankind; – Peace from the strivings in our own hearts? Do you think that we shall ever find a better and fuller answer to that cry than the one which was given long ago, 'He hath made of twain one new man'? There is a Centre of Peace in the midst of this endless agitation. Dogmatists do not see it, because they put their own conclusions in place of the manifestation of a divine Person; because they think that what we want is something that we may hold, and not an Eternal God Who may hold us, and in knowledge of Whom standeth our Eternal Life.[2] Sceptics do not see it, because they are going up into Heaven or down into the deep to seek for that which is close to them. But Dogmatists and Sceptics, when they are wearied of the greatness of their way, when they have been stripped bare of their different kinds of pride, may at last meet at the same Cross. Then they may find that the manifestation of the Perfect God in the Perfect Man is the subject of all Divine Revelation; is the object of all human search; that in His Sacrifice is the Union and Reconciliation of Godhead and Manhood, and therefore of those elements in men which are discordant, so long as we feel that God is at a distance from us, and that all our seeking for Him is not the consequence of His seeking for us.

Sermons, pp. 149–54

Notes

1 Isaiah 6.5.

2 A quotation from one of the collects for Morning Prayer in the Book of Common Prayer.

4

The Sacrifice of Christ

Consistent with his understanding of the doctrine of the Incarnation as the focal point of history, and key to the understanding of human nature, in these texts Maurice interprets the redemption wrought by Christ as flowing from his very being as one who offers himself to the Father as a living sacrifice.

On Christ's sacrifice as revealing the divine order of creation.

[The] faith of the individual man implies much more than the deliverance of his own soul. In the great annual act of atonement among the Jews, the priest laid his hand upon the head of the scape-goat and confessed over him *all the iniquities of the children of Israel, and all their transgressions and all their sins, putting them upon the head of the goat, and sending it away in the wilderness, that he might bear their iniquity into a land not inhabited.*[1] Thus the whole body of the people were taught that God, who had accepted them as a holy people to Himself, purified them, as a body, of that which had set them at war with Him. The individual Israelite could not be satisfied with his own sin-offering or peace-offering, unless he was thus assured that he belonged to a redeemed and purified society. In like manner there is no sure peace and freedom for the conscience of any one man under the New Covenant, while he thinks only or chiefly of peace and freedom for himself. The sin which he supposes he has cast aside will appear again; it will seem to him as if it was not the blood of sprinkling, but his own momentary act of faith, which had purified him from it. But if we believe that Christ has taken away the *sins of the world*, we are led to a deeper and safer foundation upon which our hopes may rest. For then we see beneath all evil, beneath the universe itself, that eternal and original union of the Father with the Son which was never fully manifested till the Only begotten by the Eternal Spirit offered Himself to God. The revelation of that Primal Unity is the revelation of the ground on which all things stand, both things in heaven and things in earth. It is the revelation of an order which sustains all the intercourse and society of men. It is the revelation of that which sin has ever been seeking to destroy, and which at last has overcome sin. It is the revelation of that perfect harmony to which we look forward when God shall gather up all things in Christ; when there shall be no more sin, because there shall be no more selfishness; when the law of sacrifice shall be the acknowledged law of all creation; when He who perfectly fulfilled that law, the Lamb that was slain, shall receive blessing and honour and glory and power;[2] when the confession of His name shall be felt and known to be the confession of the Father of an Infinite Majesty in whom He delighted, and of the Holy Ghost the Comforter, who proceedeth from them, and with them is worshipped and glorified for ever.[3]

DS, pp. 193–4

God shows himself fully in the sacrifice of Christ.

When St. Paul preached Jesus Christ, and Him crucified,[4] he preached that in obedience, humiliation, sacrifice, dwelt the might conquering power, that power against which no other in earth or heaven could measure itself. And his words have not been confuted by the experience of ages; they have been confirmed by the facts which seem at first sight most at war with them. Do you ask why the soldiers of Islam, in the first centuries after Mahomet, or in any subsequent centuries, prevailed against those who had the sign of the Cross on their banners? The only answer that can be given is, that there was more of this thought or mind of Christ, more of humiliation and obedience and sacrifice in them, than there was in their opponents. They prevailed, not through their denial of Him, but through their implicit recognition of Him. So far as they had zeal, faith, union, so far as they sought to magnify God's name, and to give up themselves, they were His soldiers, not the Prophet's, they succeeded because the Incarnate Son of God was highly exalted, because there was a name given to Him which is above every name.[5] Because all power was given Him in heaven and earth, He would not suffer those who called themselves His servants to blaspheme His Father, and to corrupt His brethren. Go through the history of the world, of the Church, of individuals, you will find it the same. So long as you creep along the ground, and ask why this man, this party, or this faith overcame, and what was subdued, you may be continually disposed to doubt and to arraign the Providence that directs all things, to charge God foolishly. But ascend above the mists of earth to the clear heaven where

Christ sits at the right hand of God, and the eternal Law becomes manifest which brings these discords into harmony. The Will that rules the universe, the Will that has triumphed and does triumph, is all expressed and gathered up in the Lamb that was slain. Beholding Him, you see whence come the peace and order of the world, whence comes its confusion. The principle of sacrifice has been ascertained once and for ever to be the principle, the Divine principle, that in which God can alone fully manifest His own eternal Being, His inmost character, the order which He has appointed all creatures, voluntary and involuntary, to obey.

DS, pp. 219–21

To 'Q', 23 August 1860.

. . . Every year and day convinces me more that our preaching will be good for nothing if the main subject of it is not the atonement of God with man in Christ – if we may not proclaim His sacrifice as a finished work; if we may not ground all our sacrifices upon it; if we stop short of the Eucharistic proclamation that God of His tender mercy hath given us His Son to be a full, perfect, and sufficient sacrifice, oblation and satisfaction for the sins of the whole world.[6] Any notions, theories, practices, which interfere with the fulness [*sic*] of this Gospel deprive men, it seems to me, of a blessing which has been bestowed upon them and to which they have a right – deprive them of the only effectual foundation for social and individual reformation.

What I say of preaching, I say also of prayers. If they are separated from the confession and presentation of the perfect Sacrifice, once made – if they are not petitions that the will which is expressed in that sacrifice may be done on earth as it is in Heaven, if they are not presented through the High Priest and Mediator within the veil – they are, in my judgment, not Christian prayers. I say not that they are ineffectual; for it is He who makes prayers effectual which are very dark and ignorant (otherwise what would become of us?); but I say that they are anticipations of a Gospel – attempts to reach an unknown, unrevealed God – not derived from the Gospel of God, from the revelation of the perfectly righteous and loving Being in the perfect Mediator.

Starting from these premises, I am bound to say that I do look upon many of the most popular statements respecting the Atonement, as interfering with the fulness [*sic*] of this Gospel, as interfering with the finished work of Christ, as robbing an immense portion of mankind of the blessing which the Bible declares to be theirs, as having the effect of inverting prayers, of divorcing them from Christ's sacrifice, of changing them into petitions that God's will should not be done, but should be changed. I look upon these popular notions as exceedingly natural, as embodying thoughts and feelings which every man ought to be acquainted with in himself, and to deal most tenderly with in others, as containing elements of old pre-Evangelical philosophy which all students and divines ought to be familiar with; but as forming no part of the message from God to man, except so far as that message meets all the confused speculations and anticipations of the human heart, and satisfies its inner cravings after God, and its secret testimonies respecting Him, by sweeping away the dark imaginations which it must form of Him when it creates Him after its own likeness. All notions respecting a conflict in the Divine mind between the claims of justice and mercy; all notions of the Son winning from the Father that which did not proceed from His own free, gracious will; all notions which substitute the deliverance from punishment for the deliverance from sin; all notions which weaken the force of the words, or make them anything less than the classical words on this matter, 'Lo, I come to do thy will, oh God,'[7] are, it seems to me, of this kind, subversive of the Divine Revelation, Rationalistic in the worst sense of that word, not to be countenanced or tolerated; to be avoided even at the risk of parting with words in themselves innocent and useful (provided they are not Scriptural words, which will always be found safe and sufficient); not to be played with or tampered with from any worldly calculation that the humble and meek cannot afford to dispense with them, seeing that the humble and meek crave for the pure milk of God's word that they may grow thereby, and are cruelly treated when those whom they reverence introduce any adulterations into it; or from any equally worldly calculations that those who doubt or deny the Atonement will take courage from the effort to separate the Gospel and the Church message concerning it from the elements which have defiled it, seeing that these elements are the great justification of their unbelief to the consciences of the sincere, seeing that those who merely cultivate unbelief as a profession, hate nothing so much as these efforts to distinguish, and as those who make them. These are my convictions, which have grown stronger and stronger in me every day, so far as the grandeur and necessity of the divine Atonement has been more manifested to me; weaker and weaker so far as I have lost sight of it, or have not given thanks for it. They have been accompanied by an ever deepening feeling that the danger of this age as of all previous ages – of the age in which our Lord dwelt on earth in human flesh most conspicuously – is not chiefly from those who consciously or unconsciously depart from orthodoxy; but from those who make orthodoxy an excuse for denying the Union of the Father with the Son, the perfect Manifestation of the Father in the Son; the desire of the Father and the Son by the Spirit to bring all men into the obedience of the Truth. I have therefore been found, and by God's grace I hope still to be found (when I am obliged to fight) fighting always against the popular not the unpopular men of the day . . .

Life, II, pp. 364–7

On the Atonement.

The broad, simple Gospel, that God has set forth His Son as the propitiation for sin, that He has offered Himself for the sins of the world, meets all the desires of these heart-stricken sinners. It declares to them the fulness [*sic*] of God's love, sets forth the Mediator in whom they are at one with the Father. It brings divine Love and human suffering into direct and actual union. It shows Him who is one with God and one with man, perfectly giving up that self-will which had been the cause of all men's crimes and all their misery . . .

I do not deny that besides these leading convictions which take possession of the heart as it contemplates the Cross of Christ, there are others apparently of a different kind. Since nowhere is the contrast between infinite Love and infinite Evil brought before us as it is there, we have the fullest right to affirm that the Cross exhibits the wrath of God against sin, and the endurance of that wrath by the well-beloved Son. For wrath against that which is unlovely is not the counteracting force to love, but the attribute of it. Without it love would be a name, and not a reality. And the endurance of that wrath or punishment by Christ came from His acknowledging that it proceeded from love, and His willingness that it should not be quenched till it had effected its full loving purpose. The endurance of that wrath was the proof that He bore in the truest and strictest sense the sins of the world, feeling them with that anguish with which only a perfectly pure and holy Being, who is also a perfectly sympathising and gracious Being, can feel the sins of others. Whatever diminished his purity must have diminished his sympathy. Complete suffering with sin and for sin is only possible in one who is completely free from it.

But is the clergyman who preaches this gospel, and sees the effect of it upon some of his flock, therefore bound to adopt those conclusions respecting the reasons of Christ's death which have so shocked the conscience of the sceptic whom he is condemning? Properly speaking, his business is simply to proclaim the good news of reconciliation. Reasons many occur to him besides those which the Bible gives us. Some may be plausible, some may be tolerable. But they do not belong to the essence of his commission. Woe be to him if he mistakes the best of them for that which it tries to account for. Since, however, it is inevitable that his understanding and imagination will be busy with this and every other subject, divine or human, that he handles, it is very necessary that he should perceive what conclusions of theirs may contradict the truth which God has committed to him. For this purpose I would beseech him to observe carefully which portions of his statements come home to the hearts of the really humble and contrite – which afford delight and satisfaction to the conceited, self-righteous, self-exalting men and women of his flock, who in ease and health think that they are safe, because they are condemning others, who in sickness and on a death-bed discover that in seeming to believe everything they have actually believed nothing. This comparison if it is faithfully pursued, and never separated from self-examination, will lead him, I believe, to precisely the same result at which he would arrive by the other method of considering what is demanded by the principles which Protestants and Romanists recognise in common. On this last subject I wish to speak a little more at large. I wish to show that the orthodox faith, as it is expressed in the Bible and the Creeds, absolutely prevents us from acquiescing in some of those explanations of the Atonement, which both in popular and scholastic teachings have been identified with it . . .

. . . It is admitted in all schools, Romanist and Protestant, which do not dissent from the Creed, that Christ the Son of God was in heaven and earth, one with the Father, – one in will, purpose, substance; and that on earth His whole life was nothing else than an exhibition of this Will, an entire submission to it. There is no dispute among orthodox people about this point, more than about the other. And there is no dispute as to the principle being a fundamental one – that on which the very nature of Christ's sacrifice must depend, as the writer of the Epistle to the Hebrews declares that it does. What we have a right to insist on is, that no notion or theory shall be allowed to interfere with this fundamental maxim. If we would adhere to the faith once delivered to the saints, we must not dare to speak of Christ as changing that Will which He took flesh and died to fulfil . . .

. . . [Scripture gives us reasons] for the Incarnation and the death of Christ. He shared the suffering of those whose head He is. He overcame death, their common enemy, by submitting to it. He delivered them from the power of the Devil. All orthodox schools, in formal language, – tens of thousands of suffering people, in ordinary human language, – have confessed the force of the words. Instead of seeking to put Christ at a distance from themselves, by tasking their fancy to conceive of sufferings which at the same moment are pronounced inconceivable, they have claimed Him as entering into their actual miseries, as bearing their griefs. They have believed that He endured death, because it was theirs, and rose to set them free from it, because it was an evil accident of their condition, an effect of disorder, not of God's original order. They have believed that He rescued them out of the power of an enemy by yielding to his power, not that He rescued them out of the hand of God by paying a penalty to Him. Any notion whatever which interferes with this faith; any explanation of Christ's suffering which is put in the place of the Apostle's explanation, or does not strictly harmonise with it; far more any that contradicts it, and leaves us open to the awful danger of confounding the Evil Spirit with God, – we have a right to repudiate, as unorthodox, unscriptural, and audacious . . .

. . . Supposing all these principles gathered together; supposing the Father's will to be a will to all good; – supposing the Son of God, being one with Him, and Lord of man, to obey and fulfil in our flesh that will by entering into the lowest condition into which men had fallen through their sin; – supposing this Man to be, for this reason, an object of continual complacency to His Father, and that complacency [i.e. 'pleasure'] to be fully drawn out by the Death of the Cross; – supposing His death to be a sacrifice, the only complete sacrifice ever offered, the entire surrender of the whole spirit and body to God; is not this, in the highest sense, Atonement? Is not the true, sinless root of Humanity revealed; is not God in Him reconciled to man? Is not the Cross the meeting-point between man and man, between man and God? Is not this meeting-point what men, in all times and places, have been seeking for? Did any find it till God declared it? And are we not bringing our understandings to the foot of this Cross, when we solemnly abjure all schemes and statements, however plausible as implements of declamation, which prevent us from believing and proclaiming that in it all the wisdom and truth and glory of God were manifested to the creature; that in it man is presented as a holy and acceptable sacrifice to the Creator?

TE, pp. 120–6

Notes

1 Cf. Leviticus 16.21.

2 Cf. reference to Revelation 5.13.

3 There is an allusion here to the Nicene Creed.

4 Cf. 1 Corinthians 2.2.

5 Cf Philippians 2.9.

6 This is a quotation from the prayer of consecration in the Communion rite of the Book of Common Prayer.

7 Hebrews 10.9.

5

The Holy Trinity

Though Maurice's understanding of the doctrine of the Trinity was not strictly original, it contained various significant and, for his age, unusual emphases. One was on the relational character of the Trinity: it was, for Maurice, a communion of persons that modelled the nature of the ideal earthly family, and in turn drew each individual believer into a special and personal union with God. Thus the doctrine of the Trinity expressed for Maurice the essentially social character of human life before God. Another was on the 'name' of the Trinity – the baptismal symbol of Father, Son and Holy Spirit – as indicating the ground of human existence.

On the Trinitarian name.

Now, if the Name into which we Europeans have for so many centuries been baptized be, as we believe it is, that which brings all these thoughts at one . . . raising them to Heaven, and yet establishing a more direct and intimate connexion between them and all the daily transactions of this earth; are we guilty of fencing men off from our Communion by a strange dogma of which they can know nothing, when we tell them that this Name is to go with them from their cradle to their grave; that the grace, the love, the fellowship of this name are to be with them as charms against all perils, light in all darkness, comfort in all sorrow; that it is to bind them with that which was in the beginning, is now, and ever shall be; that every homely duty, every act of self-sacrifice, every deed of mercy, will make the vision of it more bright, as that vision will be clouded by every act of sin, every proud thought, every uncharitable feeling; that the more they cleave to this name, the less they will dream of selfish rewards, the more they will long for the day when the sunlight of God's countenance may gladden the whole creation; that the communion of the Father and the Son in one Spirit, as it has been the ground of all their thoughts and hopes, so will be the consummation of them all, to those who shall wake up in the same likeness, and be satisfied with it?

KC, 2nd edn, I, pp. 330–1

The Trinity as the answer to human longings.

Here is the name which men in all ages had been trying to utter, of which some had muttered one syllable, and some another. These asked for an absolute, self-concentrated Being; those, for one who could hold communion with them; others for an Inspirer to dwell in them. All were divided, broken, incapable of fellowship, drawn apart by that which should have held them together, yet sure that they could be held together in nothing else. This was the name which the Father who had been seeking men to worship Him in spirit and in truth, had been educating them to know; the Name with which, when the Son had been glorified, and the Spirit had descended on different kindreds, and tribes, and tongues, people of every race might be sealed; their highest spiritual treasure, near to each – common to all. And here the absolved spirits, delivered from material notions, from sensual apprehensions – the united family have prayed together – those whose lips have been opened, whom God has helped out of their ignorance and darkness, can feel the reconciliation of their awe and their sympathy, of their sense of distinctness and their sense of Oneness, of Him whom the Heaven of Heavens cannot contain, and of Him who dwelleth in the humble and contrite heart. To discuss all notions and theories concerning this Name in the schools is easy, but to utter it in worship, O how difficult! Difficult not to the Reason which confesses the Name, and glories in it, and bows to it; but to the heart, through want of meekness, of purity, of charity. Our pride of ourselves and contempt of others, and unbelief in the largeness of God's grace, these cause the ascription to die upon our lips; these confound the Persons and divide the Substance more than all errors of the understanding. A divided Church cannot give glory to the Father, and to the Son, and to the Holy Ghost. If we dare to speak it, the Gloria must be turned into the prayer, 'Unite our hearts to fear thy Name.'

PBLP, pp. 57–8

From the chapter, 'On the Trinity in Unity' in the Theological Essays.

. . . [When] a man remembers that holiness in its fullest sense, holiness as involving truth and love, by involving separation from what is false and unlovely, must be the innermost nature of God, he may well wonder and tremble while he hears that of this it is the will of God to make him partaker. This gift is so amazing, so essential, that he is utterly baffled when he tries to meditate how he can ever be possessed of it. Can he become a God? While he dreamed of God as a being of mere power, he might dream also of measuring his own power with His. But as soon as the belief of God's holiness has at all entered into him, his desire is to sink rather than to rise. The consciousness of his pride is that which alarms him most. And that pride haunts him perpetually. If he became the most abject of men, he feels as if he should be proud of that abjectness, – more proud than he had ever been before. This is a perplexity concerning himself; there is another concerning God. It is wonderful that the inmost life of God should be communicated; but it would be a contradiction that it should not be communicated. We cannot think of a Being of perfect love as wrapt up in Himself, as dwelling in the contemplation of His own excellence and perfection: we can as little think of His being satisfied with any lower excellence or perfection. The belief of a Spirit proceeding from the Father and the Son meets both the human and the divine difficulty. To think of the Father resting in the Son, in the deepest sense knowing the Son, and of the Son knowing the Father, we must think of a uniting Spirit. And if there is such a Spirit, it must be capable of being imparted. And if this gift comes to men through the Son, we are sure that the Spirit which they receive must be the Spirit of lowliness, and meekness, and obedience. We are sure that it cannot be a Spirit which exalts any one man above his fellow. It must bring all to a level. In so far as they confess that it is meant to make them Sons of God; in so far as they confess that it is the Spirit of Christ, they confess that it is meant to make them brothers. But the more this Spirit quickens them, the more they will delight to own it as distinct from them; the more our Lord's words respecting a Comforter will seem to them the truest and fullest of all; the more they will be compelled to feel that there is a Divine Person with them to whom they owe reverence and worship.

So wonderfully, – if our baptismal faith is true, – are Divinity and Humanity blended; so awfully are they distinguished. Each step in the revelation of the distinct Persons comes out to meet and satisfy some infinite need of man; some witness which has been awakened within him of his own grandeur, and of his own weakness; of his belonging to a society, and of his being an individual; of his dwelling in a world, subject to all the accidents of time; of his right to a state that is free from these accidents. The more near he is brought to God, the greater he feels is the necessity for adoration and worship; while he contemplates Him at a distance there is terror, but not reverence or awe . . .

. . . We say that in Christ the Trinity is revealed substantially. It is not a doctrine, unless it is more than a doctrine. Either real Persons are declared to us, or nothing is declared about those Persons. Either a real Unity is declared, or nothing is made known to us about a Unity. Supposing philosophy to have perceived a Trinity, or the shadow, or the hint of one, it cannot appropriate this perception to itself, – any more than Gravitation is a truth which Newton could appropriate to himself. The philosopher must ask to what reality the perception or intuition corresponds; of what substance that which he sees is the shadow. No one is bound to assume the position of a philosopher; few have any call to assume it; but supposing a man becomes one, this must be the condition of his work: – he must seek for that which is human and universal; for Truth itself, not for some image of it, or some logical expression of it. And he must ask how truth in this sense, – truth as the equivalent of substance or being, – can be made known, so that all shall be partakers of it. I leave that thought to the modern Unitarian philosopher. I would not have him abandon his task, if he thinks that he is appointed to it. I would have him pursue it steadily. For I believe he will find that the philosopher must ascend to knowledge by the same steps as the man; that if he is to find truth, God must reveal Himself to him . . .

. . . My great desire has been to show that we are dwelling in a Mystery deeper than any of our plummets can fathom, – a Mystery of Love. Our prayers are not measured by our conceptions; they do not spring from us. He who knows us teaches us what we should pray for, and how to pray.

TE, pp. 362–70

6

Eternal Life

Maurice's teaching on eternal life was amongst the most distinctive and – in his day – notorious aspects of his thought. He is at pains in the following texts both to deny the materialism which he felt had crept into popular preaching, with its idea of rewards and punishments, and at the same time to assert the essential orthodoxy of his argument that eternal life began in the faith of the believer, and could not be subsumed under time-bound concepts of duration. To suppose that God is a vengeful God is, for Maurice, a contradiction to the Christian vision of God; rather, punishment follows from the sinner's wilful separation from the love of God.

To F. J. A. Hort, 23 November 1849[1].

My Dear Sir,

Perhaps I shall best show my interest in the subject which is occupying your mind, and my gratitude for your confidence, if I tell you something of the processes of thought through which I have myself passed, while endeavouring to arrive at the truth.

I was brought up in the belief of eternal restitution; I was taught that the idea of eternal punishment could not consist with the goodness and mercy of God. When I came to think and feel for myself, I began to suspect these determinations. It did not seem to me that the views I had learnt respecting sin accorded with my experience of it, or with the facts which I saw in the world. I had a certain revolting, partly of intellect and partly of conscience, against what struck me as a feeble notion of the Divine perfections, one which represented *good nature* as the highest of them. Nor could I acquiesce in the unfair distortions of the text of Scripture by which, as I thought, they justified their conclusions; for I had always learnt to reverence the Scriptures, not to set them aside. I did not see how *αιωνιοξ* [aionios – 'everlasting', 'eternal'] could mean one thing when it was joined with *κολασιξ* [kolasis – 'punishment'], and another when it was joined with *ζωη* [zoe – 'life'].

I do not mean that these were very deep, vital *convictions*; they were honest *opinions* as far as they went, though mixed with much intellectual pride. I despised the Universalist and Unitarian as weak; I do not know that I found anything at all better.

When I began in earnest to seek God for myself, the feeling that I needed a deliverer from an overwhelming weight of selfishness was the predominant one in my mind. Then, I found it more and more impossible to trust in any Being who did not hate selfishness, and who did not desire to raise His creatures out of it. Such a Being was altogether different from the mere image of good nature I had seen among Universalists. He was also very different from the mere Sovereign whom I heard of amongst Calvinists, and who it seemed to me was worshipped by a great portion of the religious world. But I thought He was just that Being who was exhibited in the cross of Jesus Christ. If I might believe His words, 'He that hath seen me hath seen the Father;'[2] if in His death the whole wisdom and power of God did shine forth, there was One to whom I might fly from the demon of self, there was One who could break his bonds asunder. This was and is the ground of my faith. The more I have thought and felt, the more has the Scripture met my thoughts and feelings, by exhibiting God to me in Christ, reconciling the world to Himself; the more I have been sure that I was meant to trust this Being absolutely, universally – that my sin was *not* trusting Him. The certainty of one absolute in goodness whom I could call father, has more and more obliged me to believe in a Son, to believe Him, as the Church believes Him, to be consubstantial with the Father; the more have I recognised the impossibility of a perfect all-comprehending unity, or of any living fellowship between me and my fellow-men, or of any practical faith in myself unless I confessed a Spirit proceeding from the Father and the Son, distinct from them, perfectly one with them.

I can say, I did not receive this of man, nor was I taught it. Every glimpse I have of it has come to me through great confusions and darkness. With it has come the belief that God has redeemed *mankind*, that He has chosen a family to be witnesses of that redemption, that we who are baptised into that family must claim for ourselves the title of sons of God, must witness to others that they have a claim to it as well as we.[3]

You may think I am going a long way round to get at your question; but I really know no other road. The *starting-point* of the Gospel, as I read it, is the absolute Love of God: the *reward* of the Gospel is the knowledge of that love. It is brought near to us by the Gospel, so the Apostles speak; the kingdom of God is revealed to men; they are declared to be inheritors of it. The condemnation is declared to be choosing darkness rather than light, 'hating Christ and the Father.' A rebel state of will, at war with God, is the highest, completest [*sic*] misery. So far I think all go, in words at least. All will admit that damnation is in some sense loss of God's presence, that the curse lies in the rejection of love, separation from love, abandonment to self. All admit that God has sent His Son to save us from this perdition; from every other as included in this or the consequent of it.

St. John repeating our Lord's most awful prayer takes me a step further. 'This,' he says, 'is *eternal life*, that they may know thee the only true God, and Jesus Christ whom thou hast sent.'[4] At first we shrink from the strict meaning of these words. We suppose they do not mean that eternal life is the knowledge of God, but only that those who obtain that knowledge or that life will retain it through eternity. But when I ask myself, 'Do I then know what *eternity* is? Do I mean by eternity a certain very, very long time?' I am shocked and startled at once by my want of faith and want of reason. Our Lord has been training us by His beautiful, blessed teaching to see eternity as something altogether out of time, to connect it with Him who is, and was, and is to come. He has been teaching me that I have a spirit which cannot rest in time, which must strive after the living, the permanent, the eternal, after God Himself. He has been telling me that He has come to bring me into this state, that He is the way to it. How dare I then depart from His own definition? How dare I impute my own low meaning of 'eternal' to Him, and read myself into His words, when He is raising me to another meaning infinitely more accordant with the witness of my conscience, not involving the contradictions which my own does?

Now, believing from my heart that the words in the twenty-fifth of St. Matthew are quite as much our Lord's words as those in the seventeenth of St. John, I am bound by reverence to Him – and if not by that, even by ordinary philological honesty – to apply to the former the meaning which I have learnt from the latter, this being the strictest I can get. I am bound to apply that meaning to both cases in which the word is used, getting rid of the difference which our translators have (not honestly, or with great carelessness) introduced between 'everlasting' and 'eternal'. I am bound to believe that the eternal life into which the righteous go is that knowledge of God which *is* eternal life: I am bound to suppose that the eternal punishment into which those on the left go, is the loss of eternal life – what is elsewhere called 'eternal death.'

Now, if you ask me on the strength of this passage, or of any similar one, to dogmatise on the *duration* of future punishment, I feel obliged to say, 'I cannot do so. I find *here* at least nothing on the subject. I cannot apply the idea of time to the word eternal.' I feel that I cannot; everybody feels it. What do the continual experiments to heap hundreds of thousands of years upon hundreds of thousands of years, and then the confession, 'After all we are no nearer to eternity,' mean, if not this? Do they not show that we are not even *on the way* to the idea of eternity? Might we not just as well have stopped at the hundredth year or the first? But this trifling becomes very serious and shocking, if there is a great and awful idea of eternity which our Lord would teach us, which belongs to our inmost selves, and which we are flying from by these efforts to get it into another region. For the idea of enjoying God or being without God, we unawares substitute that Mahometan felicity or Mahometan torment which you speak of, and the whole of Christianity becomes depraved in consequence.

And yet do I then dogmatise on the other side? Do I fall back on the theory of Universal Restitution, which in my early days I found so unsatisfactory? No; I find it cold and unsatisfactory still. I cannot speak of God punishing for a number of years, and then ceasing to punish, or of the wicked expiating their crimes by a certain amount of penalties. The idea of a rebel will is, to those who know in themselves what it is, far too awful for such arrangements as these. A man who feels what sin means, who feels it as the contradiction to God's nature, the perfectly holy, and blessed, and loving nature, cannot find any comfort in the thought of God leaving men alone, or hold out such a prospect as a comfort to his fellows. He feels that God is altogether Love, Light with no darkness at all. But then that which is without God, that which loves darkness, that which resists Love, must not it be miserable? And can it not fix itself in misery? Has it not a power of defying that which seeks to subdue it? I know in myself that it has. I know that we may struggle with the Light, that we may choose death. But I know also that Love does overcome this rebellion. I know that I am bound to believe that its power is greater than every other. I am sure that Christ's death proves that death, hell, hatred, are not so strong as their opposites. How can I reconcile these contradictory discoveries? I cannot reconcile them. I know no theory which can. But I can trust in Him who has reconciled the world to Himself. I can leave all in His hands. I dare not fix any limits to the power of His love. I cannot tell what are the limits to the power of a rebel will. I know that no man can be blessed, except his will is in accordance with God's will. I know it must be by an action on the will that love triumphs. Though I have no faith in man's theory of Universal Restitution, I am taught to expect 'a restitution of all things, which God who cannot lie has promised since the world began.'[5] I am obliged to believe that we are living in a restored order; I am sure that restored order will be carried out by the full triumph of God's loving will. How that should take place while any rebellious will remains in His universe I cannot tell, though it is not for me to say that it is impossible; I do not want to say it, I wish to trust God absolutely, and not to trust in any conclusion of my own understanding at all.

My duty then I feel is this: 1. To assert that which I know, that which God has revealed, His absolute universal love in all possible ways, and without any limitation. 2. To tell myself and all men, that to know this love and to be moulded by it is *the* blessing we are to seek. 3. To say that this is eternal life. 4. To say that the want of it is death. 5. To say that if they believe in the Son of God they have eternal life. 6. To say that if they have not the Son of God, they have not life. 7. *Not* to say who has the Son of God, because I do not know. 8. *Not* to say how long any one may remain in eternal death, because I do not know. 9. *Not* to say that all will necessarily be raised out of eternal death, because I do not know. 10. *Not* to judge any before the time, or to judge other men at all, because Christ has said, 'Judge not that ye be not judged.'[6] 11. *Not* to play with Scripture by quoting passages which have not the slightest connection with the subject, such as 'Where the tree falleth it shall lie.'[7] 12. *Not* to invent a scheme of purgatory and so take upon myself the office of the Divine Judge. 13. *Not* to deny God a right of using punishments at any time or anywhere for the reformation of His creatures. 14. *Not* to contradict Christ's words, 'These shall be beaten with few, these with many stripes,'[8] for the sake of maintaining a theory of the equality of sins. 15. *Not* to think any punishment of God's so great as His saying 'Let them alone.'[9]

These rules I have laid down for myself, and have tried to act upon, how imperfectly God knows. One remark I would wish to make further on this point. You speak of the Liturgy and Athanasian Creed as if they laid upon us some new burden. But they merely adopt the language of Scripture respecting eternal punishment. Whatever meaning you give it in the New Testament that you must of course give it in our services. And I am very sure that in this case, as in others, they are instruments of deliverance from the corruption and materialism of the popular theology. They do lead us to feel practically that the knowledge of God is eternal life, and the loss of God is eternal death. If we use them faithfully, we shall be educated out of the carnal into the Christian idea of eternity. Do you find that it is so with bedridden women and humble peasants? They know inwardly that Christ does not mean millions of billions of years of enjoyment by eternal life. They are not good at numeration. But they worship the Father of an infinite majesty, His honourable, true and only Son, and the Holy Ghost the Comforter.[10] Thus they find his promise made good to them, and they are not afraid of His ever ceasing to make it good to them.

You think you do not find a distinct recognition of the devil's personality in my books. I am sorry if it is so. I am afraid I have been corrupted by speaking to a polite congregation. I do agree with my dear friend Charles Kingsley, and admire him for the boldness with which he has said that the devil is shamming dead, but that he was never busier than now. I do not know what he is by theological arguments, but I know by what I feel. I am sure there is one near me accusing God and my brethren to me. He is not myself; I should go mad if I thought he was. He is near my neighbours; I am sure he is not identical with my neighbours. I must hate them if I believed he was. But oh! most of all, I am horror-struck at the thought that we may confound him with God; the perfect darkness with the perfect light. I dare not deny that it is an evil will that tempts me; else I should begin to think evil is in God's creation, and is not the revolt from God, resistance to Him. If he is an evil will, he must, I think, be a person. The Word upholds his existence, not his evil. That is in himself; that is the mysterious, awful possibility implied in his being a will. I need scarcely say that I do not mean by this acknowledgment of an evil *spirit* that I acknowledge a *material* devil. But does any one?

When I spoke in the first edition of my 'Kingdom of Christ,' of satisfaction offered by Christ to the devil, I was quoting from Bishop Hooper, and I wished to startle the admirers of our Reformers with the thought how vast a difference there must be between a theology which described the devil as demanding a price of blood, and God as demanding it.[11] I did, however, recognise a deep practical meaning in Hooper's statement. It seems to me that in sore conflicts with the tempter one may find great comfort in saying, 'Thou hast no claim on me; thou hast been paid in full measure, pressed down and running over.'[12] And if justice is done to the feeling which is implied in this language, I believe the mind is freer to receive the full idea of that satisfaction which the Son made to the Father, that perfect reflex of His own love which He presented to Him, when He gave up His soul and body to death; when He showed forth the fulness [*sic*] of the Divine love in human suffering. I cannot think there is any object so perfectly satisfying to Him who is absolutely and perfectly Love as this sacrifice. Though I see but a very little way into its meaning, I do feel that it is the atonement of God and man; and that to feed upon it must be the communion between God and man, the bond of fellowship between all creatures, the rest of each soul. In that sacrament, and in the acts of trust and charity which belong to it, we shall, I think, enter into the deepest sense of Christ's substitution – by which I mean His entire identification of Himself with our sufferings and sorrows; His intense feeling and endurance of our sins, as only One perfectly pure and loving could feel and endure them; His representation of us as the living, victorious Head of humanity at the right hand of His Father. There may be more, must be infinitely more, in it than I perceive; but this I am sure is there. If he has redeemed men from that devil and atoned them to God, He has done for us that which we need – that *is* eternal life – we may be content. And to return to that first subject, I believe that in prayers, sacraments, sorrows, works for our fellow-men, we shall see more than we can ask or think, more than all the theories in the world can enable us to ask or think, of that ransom made for all, to be testified in due time.

Life, II, pp. 15–23

On eternal life; extracts from the controversial chapter of the Theological Essays.

. . . I admit, without the slightest hesitation, that there is very much more about Eternity and eternal punishment in the Gospel than in the Law, in the words of Christ than in the books of Moses and the Prophets. Let that point be recollected and carefully reflected upon, in connection with the opinion which all in some way or other entertain, in some language or other express, that the New Testament is more completely a revelation of the Love of God than the Old is. The two assertions must be reconciled. We cannot go on repeating them both, dwelling upon them both, drawing arguments from them both, while yet we feel them to be incompatible or contradictory. Let it be further conceded at once that we cannot honestly get rid of this contradiction by attaching two different meanings to the word *αιωνιοξ* ['eternal'] in different applications. The subject which it qualifies cannot affect the sense we put upon it. If we turn it the least awry to meet our convenience, we deal unfaithfully with the book which we profess to take as our guide.

Starting from these premises, let us consider why it is that the New Testament has more to do with eternity than the Old. I think no Christian will differ very widely from me when I answer, 'It is because the living and eternal God is more fully and perfectly revealed in the one than in the other.' In both He is discovering Himself to men; in both He is piercing through the mists which conceal Him from them. But in the one He is making Himself known chiefly in His relations to the visible economy of the world; in the other He is exhibiting His own inward nature, and is declaring Himself as He is in Him who is the brightness of His glory, the express image of His person. Whenever the word *Eternal* is used, then, in the New Testament, it ought first, by all rules of reason, to be considered in reference to God. Its use when it is applied to Him must determine all its other uses . . . How can we carry out this rule? Shall we say that Eternal means, in reference to God, 'without beginning or end?' How then can we affix that meaning to Eternal, when we are speaking of man's bliss or misery? Is that without beginning as well as without end? 'Oh no! you must leave out the beginning. That of course has nothing to do with this case.' Who told you so? How dare you play thus fast and loose with God's word? How dare you fix the standard by which the signification of a word is to be judged, and reject that very standard a moment after?

But are there no better reasons why we should not affix this meaning, 'without beginning and end,' to the word *αιωνιοξ* when it is applied in the New Testament to God? I quite agree that such a meaning might have seemed very natural to an ordinary Greek. The word might have been used in that sense by a classical author, or in colloquial language, without the least impropriety. But just *the* lesson which God had been teaching men by the revelation of Himself was, that mere negatives are utterly unfit to express His being, His substance. From the very first, He had taught His chosen people to look upon Him as the *righteous* Being, to believe that all their righteousness was grounded on His. He had promised them a more complete knowledge of His righteousness. Every true Israelite had looked to this knowledge as his reward, as the deliverance from his enemies, as the satisfaction of his inmost longings, as the great blessing to his nation and to mankind, as well as to himself. His Righteousness, His Truth, His Love, the Jew came more and more to perceive, were the substantial and eternal things, by seeking which he was delivered from the worship of Gods of Time and Sense, as well as from the more miserable philosophical abstraction of a God who is merely a negative of time; *without* beginning and *without* end. Therefore, when the Son was revealed, this is the language in which the beloved disciple speaks, '*The life was manifested, and we have seen it, and we declare unto you that eternal life which was with the Father, and which has been manifested unto us.*'[13] This is but a specimen of his uniform language. Yes, and I will be bold to say that his language interprets all the language of the New Testament. The eternal life is the righteousness and truth and love of God which are manifested in Christ Jesus;

manifested to men that they may be partakers of them, that they may have fellowship with the Father and with the Son. This is held out as the eternal blessedness of those who seek God and love Him. This it is of which our Lord must have spoken in His last prayer, if he who reports that prayer did not misinterpret His meaning . . .

. . . What Aristotle was to the German in the sixteenth century [that is, a figure to battle against], John Locke is to an Englishman in the nineteenth. His dogmas have become part of our habitual faith; they are accepted, without study, as a tradition . . .

. . . When any one ventures to say to an English audience that Eternity is not a mere negation of time, that it denotes something real, substantial, before all time, he is told at once that he is departing from the simple intelligible meaning of words; that he is introducing novelties; that he is talking abstractions. This language is perfectly honest in the mouths of those who use it. But they do not know where they learnt it. They did not get it from peasants or women or children. They did not get it from the Bible. They got it from Locke. And if I find that I cannot interpret the language and thoughts of peasants and women and children, and that I cannot interpret the plainest passages of the Bible or the whole context of it, while I look through the Locke spectacles, – I must cast them aside . . .

. . . We do, it seems to me, need to have a more distinct and awful idea of eternal death and eternal punishment than we have. I use both words, *Death* and *Punishment*, that I may not appear to shrink from the sense which is contained in either. Punishment, I believe, seems to most men less dreadful than death, because they cannot separate it from a punisher, because they believe, however faintly, that He who is punishing them is a Father. The thought of His ceasing to punish them, of His letting them alone, of His leaving them to themselves, is the real, the unutterable horror. A man may be living without God in the world; he may be trembling at His Name, sometimes wishing that He did not exist; and yet, if you told him that he was going where there would be no God, no one to watch over him, no one to care for him, the news would be almost intolerable . . .

. . . Every man who knows what it is to have been in a state of sin, knows what it is to have been in a state of death. He cannot connect that death with time; he must say that Christ has brought him out of the bonds of *eternal* death. Throw that idea into the future, and you deprive it of all its reality, of all its power. I know what it means all too well while you let me connect it with my present and personal being, with the pangs of conscience which I suffer now. It becomes a mere vague dream and shadow to me, when you project it into a distant world. And if you take from me the belief that God is always righteous, always maintaining a fight with evil, always seeking to bring His creatures out of it, you take everything from me, all hope now, all hope in the world to come. Atonement, Redemption, Satisfaction, Regeneration, become mere words to which there is no counterpart in reality.

I ask no one to pronounce, for I dare not pronounce myself, what are the possibilities of resistance in a human will to the loving will of God. There are times when they seem to me – thinking of myself more than others – almost infinite. But I know that there is something which must be infinite. I am obliged to believe in an abyss of love which is deeper than the abyss of death: I dare not lose faith in that love. I sink into death, eternal death, if I do. More about it I cannot know. But God knows. I leave myself and all to Him.

TE, pp. 380–406

To another correspondent, Maurice again spelt out his view.

To the Revd D. J. Vaughan, 2 December 1853.

. . . You are quite right in your interpretation of my words. I never dreamed of merging time in eternity. The phrases which suggest such a thought belong to the popular theology and seem to me most unsatisfactory.

I maintain that *time and eternity co-exist here*. The difficulty is to recognise the eternal state under our temporal conditions; not to lose eternity in time. This difficulty which we all feel and confess, and to which preachers so continually allude, has been illustrated I think in my recent controversy with Dr. Jelf. I cannot perceive that he has ever, even for a moment, contemplated eternity as anything but the future state contrasted with the present. This mighty denial, I suppose, death will put an end to. We must some day know that we are living and moving and having our being in God;[14] we cannot always act upon the strange lie that the things which we see are those that determine what we are. But though I may speak of death as bringing us acquainted with eternity, face to face with it, I have no business, as far as I see at present, to speak of death as ending time. I do not exactly understand what that means. The eternal state I apprehend is the state of a spiritual being, out of time, living in spiritual relations, enjoying or suffering a spiritual inheritance. Its actual conditions will be determined by these, so at least I gather from Scripture, not the inward by the outward, as they seem to be (though they are not really) here.

Do I express myself intelligibly? Pray tell me if I do not; for there is nothing I desire more than to be understood by others, except to understand myself and to be understood by my Creator and Judge.

Life, II, pp. 219–20

Notes

1 Fenton Hort (1828–92), Anglican theologian and great admirer of Maurice.
2 John 14.9.
3 The unusual syntax here is indeed as in the original.
4 John 17.3.
5 This is apparently a misremembered rendering of Acts 3.21.
6 Matthew 7.1.
7 Ecclesiastes 11.3.
8 Luke 12.47.
9 Matthew 15.14.
10 Cf. The *Te Deum* in the *Book of Common Prayer*.
11 John Hooper (c.1495–1555), English bishop, martyred under Queen Mary.
12 Cf. Luke 6.38.
13 1 John 1.2.
14 Cf. Acts 17.28.

7

The Church

From his earliest published work, to his last writings, the Church was a constant theme of Maurice's. His abiding concern was to discern the lineaments of the universal Church, founded on the will of God and existing as Christ's body on earth, in the actual historical existence of the distinct elements of the Christian tradition. Often he used the term 'spiritual society' in place of the word 'church', and this expressed his conviction that the Christian Church was a community of mutual obligation, indwelt by the Spirit of God, and as such a fundamental dimension of God's ordering of the world. The Church, for Maurice, grew out of the experience of Israel, and as the worship of the Israelite people had been expressed in concrete things – the Temple, the law, sacrifice – so the being of the Church was embodied in the world in particular institutions and ordinances, in physical 'signs' including the sacraments, and in its ordering, or 'constitution'.

The Universal Church is a reality; from a letter to Thomas Acland, 12 July 1834.

. . . I would wish to live and die for the assertion of this truth: that the Universal Church is just as much a reality as any particular nation is; that the latter can only be believed real as one believes in the former; that the Church is the witness for the true constitution of man as man, a child of God, an heir of heaven, and taking up his freedom by baptism: that the world is a miserable, accursed, rebellious, order, which denies this foundation, which will create a foundation of self-will, choice, taste, opinion; that in the world there can be no communion; communion in one body by one Spirit. For this, our Church of England is now, as I think, the only firm, consistent witness. If God will raise up another in Germany or elsewhere, thanks be to Him for it, but for the sake of Germans, Dutchmen, Frenchmen, Spaniards, Italians – for the sake of Baptists, Independents, Quakers, Unitarians, for the sake of Jews, Turks, Infidels, for the sake of Men, I will hold fast by that Church which alone stands forth and upholds universal brotherhood, on the only basis on which brotherhood is possible.

We stand on the voluntary principle, we voluntarily come into God's order. We refuse to stand on the slavish foundation of self-will.

Life, I, p. 166

In language of a very different tone, in the first edition of The Kingdom of Christ *Maurice contends that the Quaker idea of the 'inner light' is essential to the true understanding of the Catholicity of the Church, and finds its fulfilment in the outward institutions and ordinances (including sacraments) of the Church.*

The principle of George Fox, the principle which you conceive to be the basis of Quakerism, is that which I recognize as the kernel of all the institutions of the Church, which leads us to the very source of its life and being. This truth, I found assailed and condemned by the English sects generally, on this plea, that it set aside, or made unimportant, the great facts of Christianity. I admitted that the charge was true, so far as it affected the promulgators of the doctrine, I denied that it touched the vitals of the doctrine itself. Here then were two parties, one asserting a great mysterious principle, as the foundation of the whole life and constitution of man, – the other asserting certain great events as essential to the scheme or plan of God; neither could come to any understanding of the other; if either prevailed, something which was most dear to the heart of the other, – something which the other felt and knew to be true, – something which those who expressly denied it implicitly recognize – must be rejected. Now it has been my object to shew [*sic*], that a body constituted by Baptism, upheld and united by the Eucharist, instructed by the written Word, preserved alive in each age by a succession of ministers, expressing its united will in acts of worship, does embody that principle, for which your Society is the witness, – does connect it with those facts, for the sake of which the other sects have rejected this principle, – does fulfil the idea of a Church Catholic.

KC, 1st edn, I, pp. 266–7

From the introductory 'Dedication' to the second edition of The Kingdom of Christ.

. . . I was led to consider the meaning of this ordinance of Baptism as a key to the nature of ordinances generally. I found that they had been much prized by Luther, and by the most earnest of those who, like him, regarded Christianity almost exclusively in its reference to their own personal life. They felt the extreme danger of substituting their belief for the object of it, and so destroying the reality of both. Their testimony was of the highest practical value, and it was abundantly confirmed to me by the experience of those who had rejected ordinances for the sake of attaining to a more spiritual state of mind. Still I could not discover how one contemplating the subject from their point of view, could ultimately escape from the conclusion which the disciples of the Reformers have so generally adopted, that he who first entertains a reverence for inward Truth, and then acquires a reverence for outward Signs, begins in the spirit and is made perfect in the flesh. And I could entirely sympathize with the feeling of Mr. Coleridge, that those who for the sake of exalting Ordinances turn them into Charms, are not making a harmless addition to that which was before sufficient, but are actually destroying its meaning and reality. But supposing them to be signs to the Race – signs of the existence of that universal body which we were inquiring after, they become invested with a very different importance. They become indispensable in a higher sense than those dream of, who seem to value them chiefly as a means of exclusion; they are the very voice in which God speaks to His creatures; the very witness that their fellowship with each other rests on their fellowship with Him, and both upon the mystery of His Being; the very means by which we are meant to rise to the enjoyment of the highest blessings which He has bestowed upon us. In this way there rose up before me the idea of a CHURCH UNIVERSAL, not built upon human inventions or human faith, but upon the very nature of God himself, and upon the union which He has formed with his creatures: a Church revealed to man as a fixed and eternal reality by means which infinite wisdom had itself devised. The tokens and witnesses of such a Church, it seemed to me, must be Divine, but the feeling of its necessity, apprehensions of the different sides and aspects of it, must, if it be a reality, be found in all the different schemes which express human thought and feeling. No amalgamation of these can create a real harmony, but each may find its highest meaning in that harmony which God has created, and of which He Himself is the centre.

KC, 2nd edn, pp. xxvii–xxviii

On the relationship of the Church and the world.

. . . St. John said there were many Antichrists in his day. It is no stumbling-block to our faith if there are many in ours. But it would be the utter uprooting of our faith if we found that there was no such body as the Apostles told us there should be, with which all lying and contention should be at war, – if there was no Spirit dwelling in that body against which these heresies and corruptions and Antichrists are fighting, and which will at last prevail against them. Romanists, Protestant nations, all sects, declare that there is such a body, and that there is such a Spirit. Their words bear witness of it; their crimes, which outrage those words, bear witness of it still more.

And thus we are enabled to understand better than by all artificial definitions how a Church differs from a world. '*The Comforter*,' our Lord says, '*shall convince the world*.'[1] When He speaks to the disciples, He says, '*He shall come and dwell in you*.'[2] The world contains the elements of which the Church is composed. In the Church these elements are penetrated by a uniting, reconciling power. The Church is, therefore, human society in its normal state; the World, that same society irregular and abnormal. The world is the Church without God; the Church is the world restored to its relation with God, taken back by Him into the state for which He created it. Deprive the Church of its Centre, and you make it into a world. If you give it a false Centre, as the Romanists have done, still preserving the sacraments, forms, creeds, which speak of the true Centre, there necessarily comes out that grotesque hybrid which we witness, a world assuming all the dignity and authority of a Church, – a Church practising all the worst fictions of a world; the world assuming to be heavenly, – a Church confessing itself to be of the earth, earthly.

From this contradiction a number of others proceed: I will take one which will serve as the specimen of a whole class. The doctrine, *Nulla salus extra Ecclesiam* ['There is no salvation outside the Church'], sounds the cruellest of all doctrines; it has become so in fact. But consider the origin of it. A man possessed with the conviction that human beings are not meant to live in a world where every one is divided from his neighbour, – in which there is no uniting, fusing principle, in which each lives to himself, and for himself, – bids them fly from that chaos. For he cries, 'There is a universe for you! Nay, more, there is a Father's house open to you. God is not the frowning, distant tyrant the world takes Him to be; not split up into a multitude of broken forms and images; not One to whom we are to offer a cold civil lip-service, by way of conciliating Him or doing Him honour. He is the Head of a family;

His Son has proved you that you may know Him as He is, not as your hard material hearts represent Him to you. Come into this Ark! Take up your place in this Family! Here is deliverance and health! *Nulla salus extra Ecclesiam.* No comfort, no health, no peace, while you count yourselves exiles from God, strangers to your brethren.'

TE, pp. 343–4

On the conception of the Church to be found in the Bible.

. . . [We] must not forget that while this universal society, according to the historical conception of it, grew out of the Jewish family and nation, it is, according to the theological conception of it, the root of both. 'That,' says Aristotle, 'Which is first as cause is last in discovery.' And this beautiful formula is translated into life and reality in the letter to the Ephesians, when St. Paul tells them that they were created in Christ before all worlds, and when he speaks of the transcendent economy as being gradually revealed to the Apostles and Prophets by the Spirit. In this passage it seems to me lies the key to the whole character of the dispensation, as well as of the books in which it is set forth. If the Gospel be the revelation or unveiling of a mystery hidden from ages and generations; if this mystery be the true constitution of humanity in Christ, so that a man believes and acts a lie who does not claim for himself union with Christ, we can understand why the deepest writings of the New Testament, instead of being digests of doctrine, are epistles, explaining to those who had been admitted into the Church of Christ their own position, bringing out that side of it which had reference to the circumstances in which they were placed or to their most besetting sin, and shewing [*sic*] what life was in consistency, what life at variance, with it. We can understand why the opening of the first of these epistles, of the one which has been supposed to be most like a systematic treatise, announces that the Gospel is concerning Jesus Christ, who was made of the seed of David according to the flesh, and marked out as the Son of God with power, according to the Spirit of holiness, by the resurrection of the dead. The fact of a union between the Godhead and humanity is thus set forth as the one which the Apostle felt himself appointed to proclaim, which was the ground of the message to the Gentiles, and in which all ideas of reconciliation, of a divine life, justification by faith, sanctification by the Spirit, were implicitly contained.

KC, 2nd edn, I, pp. 295–6

On the Church and the world again.

. . . There is another [view of the Church], which [people] suppose can be liable to no exception, which must be orthodox and Catholic. 'Christ,' they say, 'has built up a Church, has endowed it with various gifts, has pronounced it altogether good. And the world sets itself up as a rival to this divine body, is jealous of its prerogatives, wishes to enslave or to destroy it. The outward world of trees and flowers may be good enough; the things of the world, its silver and gold, may be turned to high purposes. It is the world of men from which the Church is separated, against which it exists to protest. In baptized nations she has a right to claim these men as her own. But her power over them is disputed by kings who want them as their citizens, by parents who want them to transmit their names. With these the Church finds herself in conflict. She may enter into terms with them; may make use of her services, may consent, for her own ends, to receive their honours or their wealth; but they constitute a world-order; they belong to this earth: her polity is celestial. She must always be suspecting their maxims, always devising means for exalting her own in contrast to them.' Such are the outlines of a doctrine which has been proclaimed under various modifications through every portion of Christendom; which some here as elsewhere, repeat with serious conviction; which many think that we ought to receive and believe thoroughly, if they cannot.

I will tell you why I think that, because I am a Churchman, I am bound not to receive and believe this statement, but to reject it and denounce it. The Church to which I belong, the Church which I read of in the Bible, is baptized into the name of the Father and of the Son and the Holy Ghost. This name is its foundation. But if I adopted the report of the relation between the Church and the world which this theory gives, I should be obliged to suppose that the Church had nothing to do with this Name, that it existed to contradict all which that Name expresses. For it is written, that the Father loved the world, and sent His only begotten Son into it, that He might save it.[3] It is written, that the Son came into the world, not to condemn the world, but that the world through Him might be saved.[4] It is written, that the Holy Ghost the Comforter comes to convince the world of sin, because it believes not in Christ its Saviour; of righteousness, because he is gone to the Father; of judgment, because the prince of this world is judged. The Father loves the world, the Son dies for the world, the Holy Ghost convinces the world that it has a Deliverer and a Righteous Lord, and that He has taken it out of the hands of a usurper; and the Church, which is sealed with His name, is not to love the world, not to save the world, not to convince the world, but to set itself up as a rival competitor to the world, to plot against the world, to undermine the world! . . .

This contradiction is broad and patent; it also goes down very deep . . . History tells me that when the Church has set itself up in this character, it has plotted, lied, murdered; that it has exhibited the worst qualities of a heathen society in greater concentration and intensity . . .

. . . The Universal Church, constituted in its Universal Head, exists to protest against a world which supposes itself to be a collection of incoherent fragments without a centre, which, where it reduces its practice to a maxim, treats every man as his own centre. The Church exists to tell the world of its true Centre, of the law of mutual sacrifice by which its parts are bound together. The Church exists to maintain the order of the nation and the order of the family, which this selfish practice and selfish maxim are continually threatening. And as the Church, following man's guidance, and re-constituted according to man's conception, has been enslaving, corrupting, destroying the world, and misrepresenting its Creator; so the Church, under God's guidance, obeying the principle upon which He has formed it, has been the instrument of freeing and renovating the world. The Church, exalting itself, has raised the selfishness of the world into a law, and has stamped it with divinity. The Church, humbling itself, has borne witness to the world of One who gave up Himself that He might take away its sin.

Sermons, I, pp. 281–5

In the following long extract, Maurice presents Christ as the centre of the Church's unity, and head of humanity, and indicates in a somewhat polemical passage why he thinks the Papacy is a usurpation of this centre. In the process, he identifies Protestantism as the reassertion of the principle of a national Church. This is taken from a series of pamphlets Maurice wrote in defence of the 1841 scheme for a joint Anglican-Lutheran bishopric in Jerusalem, and it contains in essence many of the key points of his argument in The Kingdom of Christ.

. . . [Men] want a Centre – they say unity without a centre of unity is a contradiction and impossibility. It must be a real Centre, not a dogma, – not a set of dogmas, whether conceived by ourselves, or transmitted by others; every institution must express and manifest this Centre; it must transcend all notions and opinions, yet it must have such a connection with the heart of man, as no notions or opinions ever can have . . . I am a Protestant just because I do acknowledge this Catholic centre, and that the moment I relinquish my Protestantism, that moment I abandon the best hope for the unity of the Church . . .

I believe then, that our Lord came into this world to set up His Church or Kingdom in the midst of it; that this kingdom is universal, unfettered by the limits of Nation or Age, of Space, or Time. I believe that this universal Church is founded on the union established between Manhood and Godhead, in the Person of JESUS CHRIST, and upon all those acts of birth, death, burial, descent into hell, resurrection, and ascension, in which His union with our race was realized, and His union with God manifested. I believe that as this union of Godhead and manhood rests, so the Church itself rests ultimately upon the name of the Father and the Son and the Holy Ghost, wherein is expressed that highest, deepest, most perfect unity, which the spirit of men in all ages has been seeking after and longing to find.

I believe that this universal Church is the only true society for men, as men – the only body which declares to us what Humanity is, and what a false, spurious, anomalous thing that *World* is, which is based upon individual selfishness, in which each man is his own centre. I believe that this spiritual and universal body was not made by Christ to depend upon the feelings, or faith of men, because these feelings and faith are nothing, unless they have something to rest on – because it is a contradiction and absurdity to suppose that they create that without which they would have no existence. I believe that He meant His Church to stand in certain permanent and universal institutions; upon a sacrament by which men should be taken into a real and not fictitious union with Him; upon another sacrament in which they might enjoy real and not fictitious communion with Him; upon creeds in which they should assert and claim their actual relationship to Him; in forms of worship wherein they should realize the highest perfection of their being, and the greatest fellowship with each other in confessing their sins to Him, glorifying His name, and asking His help; in a permanent ministry through which He should declare His will, and dispense his blessings to the whole body, and the main office in which should be that apostolic office which belongs characteristically to the new dispensation, seeing that it expresses the general oversight of Him, who no longer confines Himself to any particular nation, but has ascended up on high, that He might fill all things. Finally, in His written scripture, wherein the whole progress and development of His kingdom, is in an orderly manner set forth; its nature and constitution explained; the meaning of its ordinances, and their inseparable and eternal connection with Himself, made intelligible.

I believe that of this body, thus constituted, Christ is the everliving present Head and Centre, and that by whatsoever means this truth and principle is set at nought, by that same means each of these institutions is set at nought, its meaning and power denied, its universality destroyed. I believe that this effect, that is to say, nothing less than the disorganization and decomposition of the whole body of the Church with the loss of all its life, power, and energy, must have followed, if any of those heresies of the first ages by which Christ's Godhead or Humanity, or the unity in one person, was denied or explained away, or if any of those other heresies, by which the persons of the Godhead were confounded or its substance divided, had prevailed; and that the Church *was* dislocated and deadened just so far as they did prevail. I believe that the great teachers of the elder Church, who maintained the doctrines of the Incarnation and Trinity against these heresies, though they might speak of them as doctrines or dogmas, and might appeal to the testimony of foregone times in their support, did look upon them as great cardinal realities, as the very grounds upon which human life and human communion rest, and were convinced, that by the events of His providence, and by the course of history, God would demonstrate them to be so. I believe that though in one sense we may speak of these truths as dogmas of Scripture or dogmas of tradition, we do them and the purposes of God and our minds grievous wrong, if we do not remind ourselves continually, that they are only dogmas of Scripture and tradition, in the same sense as gravitation is the dogma of the Principia of Newton, and that they really are the grounds and laws of the moral and spiritual universe, just as gravitation is the ground and law of the physical universe. I believe that the Fathers lived and died for the support, not of dogmas, not of that which is *decreed*, of that which *seems*, but for the defence of what really *is*; for this they said that man needed to know, and this, God, after long preparation, and many gradual discoveries, had revealed.

I believe, therefore, that the truth of the Incarnation may be set aside in acts as well as words; that Christ's Headship of the Church, and the whole constitution of the Church, may be invaded by the very persons who in terms are asserting it; that a monstrous practical heresy may be introduced as the very excuse for supporting a correct dogmatical Christianity. I believe that the truth of the Incarnation, and therefore the whole constitution of the Church was invaded by an act, that a mighty practical heresy was invented for the sake of upholding that constitution, and of supporting a correct dogmatic Christianity, when the Bishop of Rome declared himself the Vicegerent of Christ and the Head of Christendom. I believe that by this declaration, the truth that a communion had been established between the visible and invisible world in the person of Christ, and that men had a right to call themselves members of Christ's kingdom, and united in him, was outraged and insulted. I believe that no human assumption or human denial can set aside an eternal truth, and that therefore that it did continue to be the fact, that Christ was the present ruler of the Church; that He was ordering its arrangements, directing its ministers, manifesting himself in its sacraments, in spite of that audacious attempt to substitute a visible and dying man in his place. But I believe, also, that this great sin was permitted to cripple every institution of the Church, and to reduce it, so far as it could be reduced, from a living form into a dead formula. I believe that it is necessary to explain to the understanding of men, how it should be possible for them to be really united to their Lord in Baptism, or to enter into real communion with Him in the Eucharist; and that for this purpose the understanding was tasked to invent barren, logical explanations, which affronted the faculty to which they were addressed, and were invested with all the sacredness and awfulness of the mystery which they degraded and profaned . . . I believe that wherever this [papal] assumption was recognized, each nation, with the king whom God has placed over it, felt itself to have an interest diverse from, and contradictory to that of the universal body; and that hence there were of necessity perpetual conflicts, contradictions, tumults, in which each side was right and each side wrong – in which the most precious and holy principles were exhibited in the most miserable condition. I believe that, owing to this assumption, it became most difficult for a common man to feel himself a true and living member of Christ's holy body, that the poor were always tempted to look upon the Church as a tremendous power overhanging them, which might crush them, and to which, therefore, they must do homage; the priest, as a machine, possessing certain invisible properties, of which he was moving the springs or wires; cultivated laymen, as a system of tricks to which they submitted one day, and at which they laughed the next.

I believe it to have been the good pleasure of God, that at the Reformation the two last of these evils which result from the headship of a visible ruler over the Church – I mean the evil to the existence of nations, and the evil to the individual soul of man – should be perceived, understood, and protested against. I believe that the distinct personal responsibility of Sovereigns to God, and that the personal responsibility of each man to God, and his need and right to claim union with Christ, in order that that responsibility might be fulfilled, were nobly and bravely asserted at that time. I believe that the assertion of these two great principles is Protestantism, because the discovery of them necessarily and inevitably led to a protest against the usurpation of the Pope over Christendom. I believe the consequence of these assertions was, for a time, the discovery of a real value in some of the great Church institutions, which had been turned into mere fictions; that the truth and grandeur of baptism were recognised; that the Creed, or at least that portion of it which refers to the acts of Christ in human flesh, was felt to be a living, and not a dead form; that the Bible recovered its glory as a living book . . .

I believe . . . that the nations of the Continent which became Protestant, became witnesses for the distinctness of nations and the distinctness of persons, but ceased to be witnesses for the existence of a universal body or family; that the nations which remained subject to the Pope of Rome continued to bear a kind of witness for the existence of such a family, but ceased altogether to be witnesses for the moral distinctness of each man, for the moral distinctness of each nation. I believe, however, that each of these witnesses was for its own purpose most weak and unsatisfactory . . . I believe that it is God's will that we should now present these great truths to men, not merely as dogmas derived from the earliest ages (though we may thank God with all our hearts that they have been so derived to us;) but in that more practical and real form in which they were presented to the men of the first ages themselves; as the solution for mysteries, for which there is no other solution; as the answers given by heaven to cries which have been sent up from earth. And I believe that this being the case, the Church, as embodied in those permanent institutions which belong to no age or nation, and which have in so wonderful a manner been preserved, may now come forth and present herself, not as a mere utterer of dogmas, which men must not dispute because they are afraid, but as the witness and embodier of those permanent realities, which earnest hearts feel that they need, and which they have been willing by God's spirit in the day of His power to receive, and which when so set forth, will be denied at last only by those who deny their own moral being and responsibility; that she may present herself not as a body, whose chief function is to banish and anathematise, but as one from which none are excluded but those who exclude themselves, because they prefer division to unity, and the conditions of a party to the freedom of an universe.

I believe, that when any part of the Church is able to assert this position, grounding its own existence simply on the Incarnation of Christ, and putting forth all those institutions and ordinances which it has in common with Christendom, as the declaration of this Incarnation and of Christ's Headship over the Church, that part of it may be blessed by God, to be the restorer of unity to the East and to the West, to the Church in France, in Spain, in Italy, in Greece, in Syria, and in Russia.

TLRWP, pp. 6–14

Notes

1 Cf. John 16.8.
2 Apparently a paraphrase of John 14.23.
3 Cf. John 3.16.
4 Cf. John 3.17.

8

The Sacraments

In an unpublished letter to Coleridge's daughter Sara, written in 1843, Maurice called the sacraments 'the transcendent language, bringing out truths full orbed of which in our . . . systems we can exhibit but one side'. This captures neatly the double aspect of his sacramental theology, according to which Baptism and Eucharist both symbolized an underlying spiritual reality or order that in some sense already existed for the believer in the providence of God and made them aware of it (a conception clearly influenced by his quasi-Platonist metaphysics), and yet also actually brought into being thereby a new dimension of that existing relationship with God. Thus, for Maurice, both symbolic and realist interpretations of the sacraments are finely (some have said precariously) balanced. What is indisputable is that Maurice's theology puts the sacraments at the very centre of Christian life, as the means by which the believer is brought into the community of the Church, and sustained in and through union with God, and that they derive their significance above all from their dependence on the prior principle of the Incarnation, the co-presence of divinity and humanity in Christ.

On baptism as admission into the visible Church, and by this means into the whole Church of God.

Maurice here addresses a Quaker friend.

[In my last letter] I maintained that Christ, by whom, and for whom, all things were created, and in whom all things consist, has made reconciliation for mankind; that on the ground of this atonement for mankind, God has built his church, declaring men one family in Christ; inviting all men to consider themselves so; assuring them that only in Christ they are or can be one family; that, separate from him they must be separate from each other. Therefore we, believing there is such an atonement, and that such a declaration has gone forth, and that it is a sin for men to account themselves separate from Christ, and separate from each other, when God has, by such a wonderful act, declared them to be one body in him; and believing that the mark of that universal body or fellowship, appointed by God himself is Baptism, do, without fear or scruple, asseverate of ourselves, and of all others who will come to this holy Baptism, of all who bear the marks and impress of that nature which Christ took, in his birth, of the blessed Virgin; that they are admitted into these high and glorious privileges; that they are brought into a state of salvation; that they are made sons of God and heirs of everlasting life; and that for this they are to give thanks to God unceasingly, and to look to Him who has introduced them to such a dignity to keep them in it even to the end. And in saying this, we contend that we give honour to the free grace and redemption of God; that we give faith, the faith of a child, the faith of the boy, the faith of the man, a ground upon which to stand, and which otherwise it cannot have. We say, hereby we are able to teach little children, that a Father's eye is upon them in love; hereby we are able to tell the young man, who is beginning to feel that he carries within him an accursed nature, which is not subject to the law of God, neither indeed can be, that by union with Christ he may rise out of that nature, and trample it under his feet; and this whether he has always maintained a fight against that nature, leaning upon the promise of his Baptism; or whether he has sunk under its dominion, and become the slave of the sin out of which Christ delivered him; for in the last case, as much as in the first, we say he must be taught that he is united to Christ; and that by not claiming that union, by trusting in himself, by thinking that he was something when he was nothing, he has become the servant of the devil, not of his true Lord; consequently, that if he would not continue in sin, he must assert that glorious privilege of which, by his own act, he has deprived himself. Lastly, hereby we enable a man, in the midst of the world's conflict and bustle, not to spend his life in fretful and selfish questionings and debatings whether he is a child of God or no, but boldly to take up the rights of one, and enter into communion with the Father; and to seek for the knowledge of God, which is eternal life; and to do his will from the heart, by his spirit dwelling in him, and to look for the manifestation of Christ from heaven, when the redeemed body shall rejoice with the redeemed Spirit, when all evil shall be cast out for ever from the kingdom of God, and when God shall be all in all.

Thus have I justified the truth which the Evangelical party assert rejecting Baptism, and cleared it of the contradictions with which it seems to me that they have encompassed it. I say you are right that Baptism is an admission into the visible church. Only understand what that implies, what it must imply, in order that your justification and your conversion may have any meaning; in order that your preaching may have a power and reality, in which now, alas! it is grievously wanting; in order that you may not be perplexed with perpetual puzzles about the degree in which you may encourage your people to believe themselves what God has declared them to be; in order that you may not keep their consciences in perpetual bondage, while you pretend to set them free; in order that you may not exalt those whom God would humble, and make those sad whom he has not made sad; in order that you may not hinder your hearers from drawing nigh to God with a pure heart and faith unfeigned, and receiving the blessings which God has promised to all who seek him.

I now turn to the High Church view of Baptism, against which, I hope, you may feel somewhat less prejudice than you did when I commenced the discussion . . .

The doctrines of this party . . . turn . . . mainly upon the principle that God, of his free will and mere grace, does, by the operation of the Spirit, in the act of Baptism, change the nature of the person partaking that ordinance, and thereby constitute him his child, the member of Christ, the heir of heaven . . .

In older and simpler times, every thoughtful man felt deep thankfulness to our Lord for the wonderful blessing which he conferred on us by teaching us the phrase *New Birth*, or *Birth from above*. To be taken out of the region of abstractions, to be presented with a fact of every day occurrence, yet still amazing and mysterious, as a key to this deeper mystery, – to be able to translate words into life, – this was exactly what every man who knew his wants felt that he needed. It was a fulfilment of the promise, that the Lord would teach his people a pure language, a language which they might interpret, not by a dictionary, but by another part of his own scheme, a part of it known to all tribes of the earth, to rich and poor, learned and unlearned alike. Therefore, understanding this to be the intent of Christ, they meditated on the obvious facts of ordinary birth, and thus they felt that their minds became clearer respecting the more transcendent truth. That the body passes from the dark night of the womb into the light of ordinary day, was the simplest view of physical birth; that the spirit comes out of the womb of nature into the light of the Son [*sic*] of Righteousness, was the corresponding view of the *New Birth*.[1] Now, in the full belief that God, by Baptism, takes the child into covenant with himself; that he adopts it into Christ's holy body; that he bestows on it his Spirit; – it was most just and reasonable that the word φωτισθεις [photistheis – 'enlightened' or 'illuminated'] should be applied to the baptised man. If he did not afterwards walk in the light, and seek fellowship with the light, he would die in his sin. But still the light is come into the world; the man is brought into the light; God himself has brought him into it; and any sinking hereafter into the dark flesh, – the womb out of which he has been brought, – is the voluntary abdication of a glorious privilege. Such is the view, I conceive, most present to the mind of the fathers of the church; and to this view, you perceive, there is nothing hostile in any of those facts respecting a passage from darkness to light in mature age, on which the Evangelical party dwell; on the contrary, one assertion rightly understood, sustains the other.

Neither is there anything contrary to what God had been previously teaching man respecting his own condition. For he had been teaching him to know that he was a spiritual creature, and that he had a nature; he had been teaching that his spirit was united to the Divine Word, that his flesh was chained to earth; he had been teaching him, lastly, that the Divine Word had claimed a union with him, and had gotten the victory over his enemies. If, then, it please God to claim the man as a spiritual creature united to Christ, and by Baptism to stamp him as such, it is pure mercy and grace indeed; but it is mercy and grace according to a Divine order; it is a mystery, but it is a mystery into the fellowship of which, God, with infinite wisdom and prudence, has been all along conducting his saints. But if for the words 'New Birth' you put 'Change of Nature,' Christ's beautiful analogy, which he has with such pains and love made known to us, is altogether set aside; for no man in his senses can find anything like a change of nature in ordinary birth. Again, the order of God is violated; he does not deal with him as he hath been doing with him; he has been preparing man, hitherto, by a wonderful process, for the kingdom of his Son, and now he sets up that kingdom on a principle of which he had given no hint before-hand. Baptism is not the consummation of a foregone scheme; it satisfies no wants previously excited, it makes useless all former dispensations. But it is a graver fault still, that by this notion the idea of a sacrament is destroyed; for in the idea of a sacrament is necessarily implied, that all the virtue and life of the creature consists in its union with a Being above itself. It is dead of itself; it lives in him. Suppose nature, as such, to become anything pure, or holy, or righteous, by virtue of any change wrought in it; or suppose a new nature to be communicated as an endowment to the man, this idea is sacrificed altogether.

I would earnestly entreat Dr. Pusey and his friends, to consider whether by this phrase they are not getting rid of a *mystery* for the sake of introducing a *mystification* . . . For, *first*, no persons are more anxious to assert the dignity and glory of the church than they, – to upset the notion that it is composed of a number of individual atoms, instead of being a Divine constitution into which men, from age to age, are brought; and yet, by representing Baptism as that which confers a portion of grace on each particular child, and not as that which brings him out of his selfish and individual condition, into the holy and perfect body, they do very much, as I think, to destroy the idea of the church, and to introduce a Genevan, individualizing notion in place of it. Secondly, no men are more anxious than they to assert the truth, that the Holy Ghost actually dwells with each baptised person; and yet, by supposing the essence of Baptism to consist in a change of nature, they make something which happens at a particular instant or crisis to the child, and not the constant presence of a Friend, and Guide, and Teacher, to uphold the spirit in its battles with the flesh, to train it in the knowledge of itself and of God, to comfort it in its sorrows, to guide it into all truth and love, – the gift and blessing of Baptism.

KC, 1st edn, I, pp. 88–96

To a lady, on the Eucharist, 3 August 1861.

If I did not believe that you and I and all people whatsoever have actually been redeemed by the sacrifice of the eternal Son of God, and that in His flesh and blood there is a new and living way consecrated for us into the presence of God, I would not urge you to frequent the Communion table. Because I do believe this and am sure that such a redemption goes beneath all thoughts, dreams, apprehensions, and that we only approach God because He has drawn us to Him, therefore I say, 'No thought about our feelings or qualifications, the amount of our faith, the consistency of our lives, the sincerity of our repentance, ought to keep us back.' We go to confess the want of feelings and qualifications, the inconsistency of our lives, and the insincerity of our repentance; we go to ask that God will give us what we have need of out of His fulness [*sic*]. But above all we want the witness and pledge of a common salvation, of a God who cares for all in Christ as much as for us. We want the plainest testimonies, those that are least dependent upon our temperament or state of mind, that He is the same yesterday and to-day and for ever.[2] The Sacrifice is His; He gives up His Son for us all. The Son went with the Father, fulfilling His will. We can but come, recollecting that perfect Sacrifice, giving God thanks that He is perfectly satisfied with us in His Son, asking to have the Spirit of Sacrifice, and that that Spirit, who is within us convincing us of righteousness, of judgment, may dwell in us and quicken us to all the good works which God has prepared for us to walk in. You will be tormented, as all are in this day, with thoughts about the meaning and extent and necessity of Christ's sacrifice. The more you connect it with Communion, the more you interpret its meaning, its extent, its necessity, by the fellowship it establishes between you and God, between you and your brother, by the only not infinite resistance which there is to that fellowship in yourself and in your brother, the more will you overcome these difficulties practically if not theoretically; and the practical conquest of this is what we need, the other will come so far as we require it. The very words which indicate the Lord's Supper, 'Eucharist' and 'Communion,' are explanatory of the whole Gospel, of our necessities, of the way in which God has satisfied them.

Life, II, pp. 393–4

The blessings of the Eucharist do not depend on holding any one particular theory about it.

But [Christ] never has scorned, and never will scorn, any one who seeks not to defend this Sacrament, or to make theories about it, but to receive it. All are invited to do that. If a man is told that the wicked are either not partakers of Christ's body at all, or are partakers of it to their own destruction, he may well say, 'Then assuredly I must not approach that table, for I am one of those wicked. My conscience tells me that I am.' But when he has arrived at that conclusion he may say further, 'Verily, I can see no way out of this wickedness, unless some one has come into the world to deliver me and my kind from it; unless some one shall enable me and all of us to be partakers of His righteousness. I hear that such an One has been: my fathers said so. Here is the Sacrament that assured them that it was so. Here is the Sacrament which told them that they might eat and live, that they might cast off the works of darkness and put on the armour of light. It speaks to me who feel the need to do that perhaps more than they did, as it spoke to them. It bids me partake of One Who died that I might live, and live for evermore. My spirit wants that food. Whether I have faith or whatever is said to be needful for that end, God knows; I leave myself in His hands. I am weary of myself; I want to be delivered from the burden of self, – I want to have that life of the Son of Man Who did not spare Himself, but gave Himself for men. It may be that I want much more than this; if I do, I believe God will give it. This I know that I want, and this therefore I will seek.'

. . . I give you instances of the way in which men may be led to apprehend the inner nature of the Sacrament, that which is most puzzling to dogmatists and theorists, by the sheerest necessity, by the experience of their own errors, of their own profoundest evil. Such persons, if they find Christ at the altar, will certainly find Him also in the study, by the fire-side, in the midst of their common work. Such men, if they worship Christ then, will gain help to preserve them from all idolatry of any outward things whatever, whether they be the elements of bread or wine, or anything else that is sacred because it is God's creature, and accursed when it is made into a God. For those who eat this heavenly food in haste because it is the Lord's Passover, with their staff in their hand and their shoes on their feet, well know that they need it to deliver them from forgetfulness of an unseen Presence, from devotion to anything visible. They have not time to speculate and debate. They want strength to live. They want to be ready for the Bridegroom, whether He call upon them to toil for Him here or to feast with Him hereafter. They want to partake of His humility because they are sure that that was in truth the greatest manifestation of His glory.

Sermons, I, pp. 17–19

The sense in which the Eucharist is a sacrifice.

. . . Some call the Eucharist a sacrifice. Some call it the commemoration of a sacrifice. Our Service is very express in giving it the latter name. We speak of the 'full, perfect, and sufficient sacrifice and oblation, which Christ made upon the cross, for the sins of the whole world.'[3] No principle is so important for us to vindicate as this. All history attests the tremendous consequences of the notion, that the sacrifice still requires to be perfected, that we are not to give thanks for it as complete. But St. Paul speaks in this chapter of a sacrifice, as implying communion, a fellowship with the Being to Whom it is offered. He speaks of the sacrifices of the Gentiles as offered to daemons or demigods (we unfortunately translate the word 'devils') and not to God; and of the fellowship of the heathen being therefore with these imperfect beings, with all their mortal and earthly passions, and not with the True God and Father of our Lord Jesus Christ.[4] This is the reason which he gives why the

Corinthians should not eat things sacrificed to idols, though they were innocent things in themselves. It implied a participation in the worship of these lower beings, an acknowledgment that men were subject to them, when Christ had redeemed them and brought them to His Father. Let us understand then, well, what this finished sacrifice has done for us; let us understand why we are to give thanks for it. If it had left us merely to the recollection of the past, it would be unlike all God's elder sacraments; for they brought the Jews, who received them truly, to recollect that He Who brought their fathers out of Egypt was with them in the promised land, with them in whatever land of exile they might be called to dwell in, and that they might offer themselves as sacrifices to God. These sacraments told them that they must not be content with the present or with the past, that God intended them for a more perfect communion with Him, that He intended to manifest Himself fully to the world. No lower belief, no feebler hope, can assuredly sustain us, upon whom the ends of the world are come. The sacrifice has been made once for all. But it has been made that we might be united to the great High Priest, Who has entered within the veil, and Who is presenting His finished sacrifice continually before His Father.[5] It has been made that we might look onward to that day, which is to wind up all the revelations and all the sacraments of God, when His servants shall see His face, and His Name shall be in their foreheads, and 'there shall be no night, and they shall need no candle, neither light of the sun; for the Lord God will give them light, and they shall reign for ever and ever'.[6]

Sermons, I, pp. 40–1

Notes

1 Cf. Malachi 4.2. Presumably the substitution of 'Son' for 'Sun' is simply a typographical error in the original.

2 Cf. Hebrews 13.8.

3 A paraphrase of the consecration prayer in the Communion rite in the Book of Common Prayer.

4 Cf. 1 Corinthians 10.14–22.

5 Cf. Hebrews 6.19–20.

6 Revelation 22.5.

9

Church Unity

At first glance, Maurice's views on church unity look much like standard Protestant argumentation that the invisible Church – the universal Church – already possesses a unity that is to be found in each of the historic churches, however great the differences between them. But Maurice's concern for Christian unity in fact went much further than this. The traditional Protestant view assumed that unity was grounded in a common faith above all, and that it need not presuppose any particular form of church order. For Maurice, by contrast, the order of the Church was certainly one vital aspect of its universality, and this order – which, as we saw above, is expressed in the sacraments, ministry, creeds, Scripture, and worship of the Church – was inseparable from its interior faithfulness to the gospel. The language of 'visible' and 'invisible' Church suggested that the particular form of visibility each church might take was a matter of indifference; for that reason he disliked it and rarely used it. The conclusion Maurice drew was that the universal Church did have a definite form, in what he called its 'constitution', and that central elements of that constitution were to be found in the positive principles affirmed by each of the main branches of Christianity. Unity subsisted, not underneath particular churches, but in them, where it was usually limited and distorted by history. By the careful study of history, Maurice suggested, Christians could begin to rediscover the truly comprehensive identity of the Church, and in turn begin to realize (in the sense of 'make real') the true unity of the Church.

Christ is the basis of church unity.

To A. J. Scott, 20 February 1839.

. . . I have endeavoured to prove in my tracts[1] that if Christ is really the head of every man, and if He really have [*sic*] taken human flesh, there is ground for a universal fellowship among men (a fellowship that is itself the foundation of those particular fellowships of the nation and the family, which I also consider sacred). I have maintained that it is the business of a Church to assert this ground of universal fellowship; that it ought to make men understand and feel how possible it is for men as men to fraternise in Christ; how impossible it is to fraternise, except in Him. Now the denial of a universal head is practically the denial of all communion in society. This universal fellowship in Christ, I believe that the Church of England asserts by its ordinances; and believing this (rightly or wrongly), I feel that *I am bound* as a good member of that Church not to narrow my terms of intercourse or fellowship. I meet men as men because I feel that I have a ground on which I can meet them, and that this is the deepest, safest ground of all. If they do not acknowledge it distinctly, or even if by their works they deny it, I may still hope in some way or other, by God's blessing, to make them conscious of it. If they do acknowledge it, and exhibit the practical results of the acknowledgment, I have as strong and full a sympathy with them as my own miserably imperfect and feeble apprehension of the truth on which we stand permits. If the person whom I thus meet fraternises elsewhere, on another principle, that is nothing to me. Still less does it signify to me that he may support in conversation certain theological theses to which I cannot assent, or may deny doctrines which I hold very earnestly. I should make no compromise, I should hope to be enabled to tell him honestly what I think, but my friendship with him would not be interrupted: or, if it were, I should attribute the breach to my infirmity of temper, and not boast of it as a sacrifice to duty. This would be my way of acting in society.

But if the same person said to me, 'Let us meet tomorrow at some meeting of the Bible Society; I am an Independent, or a Baptist, or a Quaker; you, I know are an Episcopalian; but let us forget our differences and meet on the ground of our common Christianity,' I should say, instantly, 'I will do no such thing; I consider that your whole scheme is a flat contradiction and lie. You come forward with the avowal that you fraternise on some other ground than that of our union in Christ, and then you ask me to fraternise with you on that ground. I consider your sects – one and all of them – as an outrage on the Christian principle, as a denial of it. And what is the common Christianity which you speak of? The mere *caput mortuum* ['death's head'] of all systems! You do not really mean us to unite in Christ as being members of His body; you mean us to unite in holding certain notions *about* Christ; just as you hold certain peculiar notions about baptism, the independence of congregations, &c. But you say I am an Episcopalian. It is true; I acknowledge the authority of bishops. But I do not fraternise in the belief in the authority of bishops. I would refuse the right hand of fellowship to any one who asked me to stand with him on that ground, as I now refuse it to you. If you do not understand this; if you cannot see that just as I meet Englishmen, not on the ground that I agree with them in thinking a limited monarchy the best form of government (though I may think that), but on the ground of our being Englishmen, of our having the same Queen, the same laws, the same ancestors, recollections, associations, language, so I meet Churchmen on the ground of our being Churchmen, of our having one head, of our having the same relation to an innumerable company of spirits that are on the earth and that have left the earth. If you cannot perceive this, I see more clearly than ever what your sect system has done for you; I see more need than ever of protesting against it by word and deed, in season and out of season.

Life, I, pp. 258–9

The danger of sectarianism.

To the Revd J. De la Touche, 6 April 1863.

. . . I am sure that you will find every sect narrower and more cruel than the Church. I am sure that the Church is only narrow and cruel when she apes the sects, and assumes the character of a sect.

Life, II, p. 444

Church division is a result of human sin; and therefore all who seek church unity must acknowledge their own part in this division.

. . . The great schism of the Greek and Latin Churches strikes the student of ecclesiastical records as a most startling contradiction in the history of a body which was to include all nations and races. Yet it was surely from the Lord. Idolatrous habits and feelings had been spreading in both divisions of the Church. The sense of union in an invisible Head, though not lost, was fearfully weakened. A seeming union must have been preserved by the loss of all witness for real union; the division remains a standing witness against the possibility of a visible head ever holding the Catholic body together.

The schism of rival popes in the Western Church during the fifteenth century was as great a scandal to Christendom as can be conceived. Yet it was surely from the Lord. It led men to perceive that there was corruption in the head and in the members of the ecclesiastical polity; it led to those disputes respecting the relative powers of popes and councils, which showed that neither could heal the wounds of the Church or preserve its unity. It led to that movement in the sixteenth century, – which we all I trust believe to have been from the Lord, and which was really a declaration of faith in a living God, – against a system of idolatry that was rapidly passing into a system of organised unbelief. In each of these cases there were chances of reconciliation and noisy fanatics preaching uncompromising resistance. In each case the infatuation of princes and rulers, ecclesiastical and civil, was carrying out a divine and eternal principle even when they were defying it. They could not restore unity by declamations, by concessions, or by persecution. Facts spoke louder than the Prophet spoke to Rehoboam, 'It cannot be. The thing is from the Lord.'[2]

In the last period to which I have alluded there were, in England as much as in any country, those who looked upon the new and reformed state of things merely as a means of establishing their own power; who regarded the Church as an instrument of keeping up that power; who valued a worship in their own language, not because it brought their countrymen nearer to God, but because it was a badge of separation from foreigners; who protested against the idolatry of papal nations, and were really making royalty, or the privileges of the upper classes, or money, as much objects of their idolatry, as the calves in Dan or Bethel were to the ten tribes. And therefore we must not shrink from the acknowledgment, that the different sects which rose up in this land, seemingly to rend the body of Christ more completely asunder than it had been rent already, were from the Lord. There were idolatries in the ruling body which made such divisions inevitable. The first impulses of those who began them were like those of Jeroboam, pure and honourable. They became spokesmen of hearts which were suffering under a burden; they encountered Rehoboams in the State and proud men in the Church, who said 'Let us change rods into scorpions;' compromises failed, persecutions failed; the thing was from the Lord.[3] And the lesson was repeated again in those separating bodies. Politic men rose up, who sought to make the division permanent and hopeless. The separate priest, and altar, and sacrifice must be introduced, that there might be no recollection of the bond which united them to those from whom they were severed. Hence the one sacrifice for mankind became lost in the notion of some special salvation for themselves. New forms of intellectual, if not sensual, idolatry appeared; the victims of them groaned under the narrowness and bondage, which they had been taught to call liberty. Are not many of them even now ready to turn for refuge from their sectarian faith and freedom, sometimes to the vaguest forms of unbelief, sometimes to the most perfect and universal despotism over conscience and will?

Oh, brethren! how intolerable would be these facts and recollections which show every party in Church and State to have been the cause of shameful scandals, which forbid us to cast stones at others because we are in the same sin, if we might not recur again and again to the words which I have quoted so often. But if the thing is of the Lord, there must be an end of all those strifes by which He has ordained that our idolatries against Him and cruelties to our brethren should punish themselves. There must be a day when all things in heaven and earth, which consist only by Christ, shall be gathered manifestly together in Him; when it shall be known and confessed that there is one king, one priest, one sacrifice; – that we have been at war with each other, because we have not done homage to that one king, drawn nigh to God through that one priest, omitted to present that one sacrifice. And those who are willing before God's altar to own that their self-seeking and self-will have been rending asunder their families, the nation, the Church, the world, – may hope that God's Spirit will work in them henceforth to do all such acts as shall not retard, but hasten forward the blessed consummation for which they look. They may ask to be taught the mystery of daily self-sacrifice, – how to give up their own tastes, opinions, wishes. They may ask that they may never be tempted to give up one atom of God's truth, or to dally for one moment with the falsehoods of themselves or of their brethren; because truth is the one ground of universal peace and fellowship, because falsehood and division are ever increasing and reproducing each other.

PKOT, pp. 103–6

Notes

1 A reference to the tracts that became the first edition of *The Kingdom of Christ*.

2 Cf. 1 Kings 12.23.

3 Cf. 1 Kings 12.14.

10

The Church of England

So much of Maurice's writing was prompted by controversies in and about the Church of England, that it is impossible to do more here than include a few passages that bear on his defence of his church. Following the theory he mapped out in The Kingdom of Christ, *his main preoccupation was with the way in which, in his view, the Church of England combined the features of the universal church (the 'signs' and 'ordinances') with the appeal to national independence: consequently for Maurice one of the key points about the Church of England was that it was the national Church. This is the point of his combined emphasis on the Church of England as both Catholic and Protestant. Yet its catholicity demanded, not a narrow factionalism, but a truly comprehensive vision of the Church, as in effect always much more than the mere sum of its individual members' opinions. Included here is almost the full text of his early pamphlet,* Reasons for not Joining a Party in the Church, *which demonstrates his assumption of comprehensiveness in full flow.*

The Church of England is part of the universal Church of Christ.

To Thomas Erskine, 8 August 1841.

. . . The English *Church* I look upon as merely one branch of the true Church; and every *system*, whether called Evangelical, Liberal, Catholic, or Purely Anglican, which has been invented by the members of that Church in former times and in our own day to express their notions of the Church, I look upon as 'of the earth earthy,' and as much carrying in it the seeds of destruction as the systems of the different sects which have revolted from her. The Church – it seems to me – is a part, the highest part, of that spiritual constitution of which the nation and the family are lower and subordinate parts; implied in the acts we do and the words we speak, established before all worlds, manifested as the true and everlasting kingdom when the Son of God died, rose, and ascended on high, testified as the common property and inheritance of men by certain forms and ordinances which convert it from an idea for the mind into an actual reality for all who will enter into it and enjoy it, and which prove God to be true though all men be liars. The Catholic Church, I think, has established itself in the East and the West, and is acknowledged by God as His kingdom upon earth. It has been preyed upon by diseases of all kinds in the shape of human systems: by the Romish system, which is the most successful parody and counterfeit of its Catholic character, and practically contradicts and outrages that, as well as its spiritual character; by Protestant systems which parody its distinct and personal character, and really outrage that as well as its principle – universal human fellowship. Yet in spite of these, and other different systems which have attempted to make a middle way between them, and so, I think, to combine the mischiefs of both, the Church, I think, is coming forth, and will manifest itself as something entirely distinct from them all – distinct, too, from the faith which exists in the minds of those who spiritually dwell in it, though requiring it and supporting it.

Life, I, pp. 306–7

On the providential foundation of the Church of England.

. . . In what I have said [in an earlier letter], I have anticipated my answer to your charge against the English Church, that her character is ambiguous, because she calls herself both Catholic and Protestant. I have shown, I think, that she is not obliged to be half Catholic and half Protestant, – not obliged to chalk out a middle way, in the sense which you give to that phrase; but that it is possible for her, or for any other portion of the Church, to be most Catholic when she is most Protestant. Still, I think it important for the comfort of our own consciences, and for the right understanding of our relations to others, that we should examine more carefully what our position is; what acts of ours might be more inconsistent with it; what acts might show our gratitude to God for it.

. . . [Those] institutions were preserved to us at the time of the Reformation, which do not belong to us as individuals, or as members of a nation, but as members of a Christendom . . . I believe the English Reformers to have been in mind and spirit like the foreign Reformers, occupied mainly with questions concerning national and individual life, very little with considerations respecting the being and order of the Universal Church. Whatever feelings they had upon this last subject had come to them traditionally, or were the accidental accompaniment of other feelings rather than the radical and governing portions of their mind. I do not therefore claim for them more than a passive acquiescence in, and submission to, that will of God, which directs our ends, even when we are disposed to rough hew them. I do not seek to exalt the English Reformers, by claiming for them a particular wisdom and excellence which were wanting in their contemporaries abroad. I am not ashamed to say that I admire both very sincerely, because I believe that, amidst a great many errors and sins, they followed the leading of God's providence, keeping their eyes fixed upon that object upon which, in their time, and under their circumstances, it was right and fitting that they should be steadily, almost exclusively, fixed . . . I do not claim for the Reformers the merit of preserving Catholic institutions among us; it is altogether a wonder that they should have been preserved, and as a wonder I would receive them, and give thanks for them.

But, secondly: These institutions have come down to us clogged with a protest against the Bishop of Rome. That protest was made not less strongly, but more strongly, by our Church, than by those from whom she derived it; more strongly, because it was the effect of no sudden start of individual feeling. The protest against the Romish usurpation over the rights of sovereigns had been going on for centuries; the only difference was, that this came into coincidence with the individual protest which had hitherto been denounced and kept down, and that as the one was put forth by the sovereign himself, the other was adopted by a great portion of the Bishops and Clergy. And thus it has come to pass, that if we inherit a church, possessing all Catholic institutions, we inherit a church, which is subject to this protest – which made it once, and is making it now. Our Bishops declared that they had a spiritual authority independent of the Bishops of Rome. They exercised that authority in condemning the theory of the Eucharist, which he had pronounced to be necessary to it, and necessary to salvation. They renounced the innovations which the Bishop of Rome had sanctioned in the old liturgies; they used their own discretion in arranging the old forms, and even in introducing new forms; they did acts of homage to the king as, over all causes ecclesiastical and civil within his own dominions, supreme . . . We are therefore a protesting church. I do not use the words because I wish to urge upon any person, who disapproves the protest, the duty of leaving her; I believe that it may be, and in nine cases out of ten it is, a very solemn duty for us to remain in the church wherein we are born, though we dislike many of the conditions under which she exists; and I have no sympathy whatever with the language about dishonesty and inconsistency, which certain writers among us so readily and wantonly use. But I wish simply to state facts. We may cease to be Protestants, but at present we are Protestants, and have been so for the last three hundred years . . .

A third point must be distinctly taken notice of, though it has been touched upon lightly. If our Church is both Catholic and Protestant, our Nation is wholly Protestant. In so far forth as we are a nation, united together under one king, we do by the very law of our existence protest against any power which assumes control over our kings, and denies their direct responsibility to God. The nation's position is, and always must be, a protesting position. Whether it follows as a matter of course that a nation and a church are incompatible with each other, that one must perish if the other is to live, is of course the very question in debate between us. I believe that the nations were brought into their distinct life by the church – that they cannot retain their distinct life without the church; and that conversely, the universal body sinks into a contradiction, when it refuses to recognise the personality of each national body. Be that as it may, the question as to England is one of history, and not one of speculation. We are not striving to make ourselves a Protestant nation now: we have been so implicitly at all times; explicitly since the Reformation.

TLRWP, pp. 16–19

On the impact of the Oxford Movement, and its errors in supposing Anglicanism should cease to be Protestant.

. . . The English writers, to whom [the Tractarians] appealed as their forerunners and authorities, were in the strictest sense English;[1] though they might hereafter expect a union with other parts of Christendom, their main purpose and interest was to assert the peculiarities of the Anglican Church. By whatever names, therefore, they might be called, they were vehemently Anti-Romanist, as well as vehemently Anti-Lutheran. But those who adopted them as their guides, had been led into quite a different state of feeling from this; they were carried on, though they knew it not, by that great Catholic movement which all parts of Europe have experienced; their ground of admiration for those institutions which were preserved in the English Church, was not that they were English, or even ancient, but that they were Universal. I say they were not conscious of this fact themselves, and therefore they said with great simplicity, that they wished to be Anglicans and nothing else. But it was quite impossible, in the nature of things, that they should continue to feel thus. It was quite impossible that the more earnest and the better part of them could look upon those elements in our life, which are especially to connect us with all people, merely as barriers, to banish and exclude . . . They began to open their eyes to the fact previously hidden from them, that people elsewhere were craving after Catholic union as well as themselves; that, in fact, it is the desire which God is bringing out in men of this age, and which only makes itself more evident from the efforts of the evil spirit to draw them into greater conflicts and a more selfish position. Seeing this, they became impatient of their Anglicanism. They began to say, It is a very narrow, close, selfish thing after all; possibly it was a step to something better; but now that we have found the better thing, we may throw aside the step; the great point is, how we may enter into fellowship with the Church at large, the Church Catholic. Hence have grown up those desires for union, if it can be obtained, with the nations which are still subject to the Papal Hierarchy – hence, that inclination to pass over or extenuate all the faults of which that Hierarchy has been guilty – hence, that craving after a visible centre of unity, by which honest persons, who, as they express it, 'had gone a certain way with the Oxford School,' have been startled and scandalized, and which have given its bitterer opponents an excuse for saying, that its members concealed their opinions under a specious national form, till the time was come for fully disclosing them. . .

. . . [We] may derive, I conceive, great instruction from the lessons which the history of this school affords us. It began with asserting that we have a peculiar English position to maintain, different either from that of the Romanists or of the Continental Protestants: is not the assertion plainly and obviously true? It has discovered at last that we cannot make the possession of certain universal blessings a mere national boast, that they ought to be our bonds with other nations: is not this assertion true also? They are rapidly throwing aside all Anglican and national feeling. Do not our hearts and our consciences tell us that they are thereby sustaining a grievous loss, that they are destroying links of affection which subsist between them and other generations, that they are cultivating tastes and preferences of their own – a sentimental attachment to foregone ages – and are parting with the actual human sympathies which might make the others not fantastic but real? Have we not then a clear indication of the truth, that the things which they would separate are really one, that the national bond and the Church bond are not incompatible, though they cannot be the same, that we may bring the two parts of our lives into reconciliation, that the one may be the helper and not the hinderer of the other?

Supposing this were so, it might still be very difficult for us to chalk out a path for ourselves; but we must believe that what we cannot effect, God's providence will, and that, by watching His providence, we may be able to guide our steps aright. Our object is clear; we are to aim at entering into communion with all Christian people, so far as we can do so without sacrificing any of those principles upon which communion itself rests. We are to desire that we may profit by all the advantages of our ecclesiastical and national position for the purpose of obtaining this communion. We are to count it a sin to sacrifice either our ecclesiastical or our national position, for the sake of obtaining it.

TLRWP, pp. 22–5

In Reasons for not joining a party in the Church, *Maurice took issue with Walter Hook, a High Churchman who had urged his fellow Anglicans to take one side or other – Low Church or High Church – in the controversy that followed the publication of John Henry Newman's* Tract 90.

Such sentiments as these scarcely require the authority which they will derive from the name and character of their author. They are exactly what a great majority of our countrymen have adopted for years. 'There is an absolute necessity to range ourselves on one side or the other;' 'we must become party-men;' 'we cannot halt between two opinions;' – these phrases are tolerably familiar to most of us. The difficulty has been to shut our ears to them, to find some other maxims upon which we might act. If I am asked why we have put ourselves to this difficulty; I answer, the motives may have been various: Experience may have taught some that they could not take a plain honest course while they were bound to follow certain leaders and adopt certain shibboleths; some may have found that course, and all the habits of service which it involves, most unfavourable to their personal character; some may have been tempted so often to change one party for another, with so little increase of peace to themselves and of good to their neighbours, that they may have at last begun to inquire whether there were no means of escaping the obligation altogether. But the one great argument, I believe, of late years, against the popular doctrine is, that the words *Party* and *Church* are essentially hostile to each other; that he who says, 'I will be a Churchman,' says, in effect, 'I will *not* be a Party-man;' that he places himself under bonds and conditions, with which those other bonds and conditions are, in principle as well as in practice, incompatible. This feeling has been growing strongly amongst us. We have been taught that Church maxims and principles are in nearly all cases opposite to those of the world; that, nevertheless, they may be followed out by those who will follow them out. It was nothing then to be told – 'This notion that Party is indispensable has a very wide currency; good men have adopted it, and are adopting it; you yourselves are continually falling into it unawares.' All this might be very true; but it is true of a hundred notions and practices which we are to hate and denounce, to which we acknowledge that we are prone, and from which we desire that we may be purified. And the belief that freedom from this particular anti-Church doctrine, if it may not be rather called the great anti-Church doctrine, is possible, was strengthened by the words of various persons whom we revere, though we may not, in defiance of their own commands, accept them as oracles. In his Letter to the Bishop of Oxford, Dr. Pusey repudiated the notion of belonging to a party, with the earnestness which belongs to his character and to every thing that he utters.[2] Dr. Hook delivered a sermon to the Clergy, which was from first to last an eloquent and passionate 'Call to Union.'

My surprise, then, at reading these words, was not at all occasioned by their novelty; but I did feel most deep and unfeigned surprise to see from what quarter they proceeded, and by what arguments they were enforced. To be told by Dr. Hook that what I had believed – and I thought upon his authority – to be a sin, though of course a most natural sin, and one for which we were not to judge and condemn any but ourselves, was become a *duty*; and then, that this amazing change had been wrought by the vote of a Weekly Board at Oxford – this did seem to me most strange. The circumstances and obligations of the whole body of English clergy, (for the word '*us*' cannot refer merely to the clergy in the diocese of Ripon – it must mean those in the diocese of Winchester just as much; it cannot refer merely to conspicuous clergymen like Dr. Hook – it must take in the most insignificant,) are entirely altered; that which was to be avoided is to be sought; that which was wrong is right, because certain heads of houses in one of our Universities have condemned the 90th Number of the Tracts for the Times!

It seemed to me so difficult to believe that this could be the author's meaning, that I tried what my critical ingenuity could do in discovering some other. His first words, that it was impossible to conceal the *fact* of our divisions, made me hope, for a moment, that it was a *fact* of which he was speaking, and not a duty; that he wished to say, 'We are divided,' not we are under an obligation to adopt division as our law. But, then, I asked myself, 'Were we not divided before the vote of the Hebdomadal Board; or was Dr. Hook in ignorance of that fact, or did he think it one which could be safely kept secret till five weeks ago? What then was the meaning of his sermon at the Bishop of Ripon's visitation? Surely it presumed this fact, and proclaimed it to the world; for will anyone say that a grave and practical preacher would in the most solemn manner exhort his brethren to repent of a sin which he did not believe that they had committed; or would he have suffered that exhortation to go forth, if he did not believe the grounds for it to be so notorious, that it was absurd, as well as dishonest, to affect the least disguise in speaking of them?

Again, it seemed to me just possible, that Dr. Hook might intend only, by the words '*we must become party men,*' 'we must frankly declare our opinions, be they what they may.' In writing a hasty pamphlet, the most considerate person may easily adopt a phrase which in the world's dialect is equivalent to some other that he wishes to utter: he may dislike the phrase, but it cleaves to him unconsciously; nay, he may persuade himself, that it was the only one which would be intelligible to his readers. And, though such an excuse ought hardly to be pleaded, respecting a letter to a bishop; yet as that form may be taken for a discourse which others are meant to hear, there was less difficulty in admitting this explanation. But, then, I was obliged to consider again, whether this obligation of declaring what we think and believe has been suddenly imposed upon us by the Hebdomadal Board at Oxford. It has been generally supposed that there are times when silence is a man's privilege and duty; when he is to be esteemed wiser and better for not intermeddling. But this silence has been referred to a principle: we have been taught, that no honest man will suppress what he thinks, merely because it is more prudent and politic for his own sake to do so. I cannot conceive how the case has been changed by this vote. It is not, I hope and trust, everyone's duty to be speaking and writing about the Tracts for the Times; the right of silence is not to be wholly taken away. And the law, that we should speak exactly what we think, and not something else, whensoever we do speak, is surely of very old enactment. Even though no Oxford Board existed, it would be Dr. Hook's duty, if he agreed in the general opinion, that we must be party-men, to state that doctrine boldly; it would be mine, if I thought I might venture to open my lips at all, to say why I dissent from it.

I fear then that the author of the Letter to the Bishop of Ripon, must intend to retract the sentiments contained in his sermon. Union may still be a good, but it is an unattainable good. He plainly intimates, that let the theory of the matter be settled as it will, any honest person, since the recent events in Oxford, will find it practically impossible not to avow himself a member either of the High Church or the Low Church School. On this point I wish to say a few words.

I must begin with taking all objection to the names by which Dr. Hook has described these schools. Popular catchwords are nearly always deceitful; in this case they are singularly so. The phrase 'High Churchman' is most equivocal; it would be claimed by persons with whom Dr. Hook has no sympathy, and who have no sympathy with him. I do not say which has the older or better title to the name; at all events, in our generation it has been appropriated to both, but more commonly to those who care nothing for the Catholic Church, and, except in their pews on Sundays, never use the words, but in the way of reproach. The phrase 'Low Churchman' is equally inconvenient: it includes persons so opposite in feeling and opinion as Bishop Hoadly and Mr. Scott of Aston Sandford;[3] and what is worse, it describes merely the negative opinions of men who at all events believe that they hold something very positive. I would therefore venture to substitute for these names, two which these schools have respectively chosen for themselves, '*Anglo-Catholic*,' and '*Those who hold the peculiar doctrines of the Reformation*.' Mr. Newman, I am sure, would not have the slightest unwillingness to give up the latter title to his opponents: if Dr. Hook should object for a moment, I am sure he will withdraw his opposition, when the phrase is explained. He approves, we all know, of the principles of the English Reformation; but then he approves them just in those points wherein they were different from the principles of the foreign reformation. Now, by 'doctrines peculiar to the Reformation,' I mean those doctrines which were common to the English with the foreign Reformers – doctrines, therefore, which do not belong to the Catholic side of our Reformation, though, whether they be contrary to it or not, is precisely the question which I imagine is now at issue.

Adopting then this description of these two schools, as one to which neither can object, a person who believes that he cannot join either of them might give some such reason as this of his faith: – He might say, that having endeavoured to study the history of that which is called the Low Church School, he had become deeply convinced that the Protestant principles have a deep value and meaning; that they interpret to a man his own personal being; that, whenever they have been lost or kept out of sight, or merged in any others, men have become unintelligible to themselves, and have lost all sense of their distinct relationship to God; that then they must be recovered with a great struggle, and at considerable peril; but after they have been so recovered, they are felt for a time to be all-sufficing; that the generation which has embraced them with a first-love ardour, amidst much opposition and resistance, passes away, and that a new generation grows up in which they are received as household words, and become little more than phrases; that then a want is experienced of something to quicken and support them; that first it is fancied they have been too much mixed with other notions, and that they must be separated, and put forth more exclusively; that the experiment of so doing is tried and fails; that then the notion gets abroad that they are not sufficient, that other truths are necessary to satisfy men's deepest wants, – truths which refer not to man's personal life, but to the constitution of society, and the being of God; that there is a struggle in various directions to find what these truths are; that a *Catholic school* springs up to meet this necessity; that it is stoutly resisted as dangerous, and as introducing ideas which are not wanted for man's individual interests and salvation; that nevertheless its words go forth, and are heard, and that there is something in men which testifies that these ideas are needful to their inmost hearts, whether they can be brought under the head of doctrines necessary to salvation or no. From these observations, an inquirer might draw the conclusion that Protestantism cannot exist without Catholicism. He would not mean by this that it cannot exist *safely* – that it requires to be balanced by Catholicism; he would not mean this at all; but, on the contrary, that it has not its proper strength while it stands alone; that this union is the condition of its vitality. He might go on to say, that having tried to watch the progress of the Catholic school, he had noticed that it was welcomed by the deepest, humblest, most earnest minds, when it spoke of that which it seemed appointed to speak of – the law of our fellowship, the duties growing out of that fellowship, the manifestation of God, the unfathomable mystery of His being and unity; that it was resisted by the deepest, humblest, and most earnest minds, when it ventured to decide questions respecting the conscience, and whatever appertains to us as distinct individual men; that when it meddled with these matters, all its life, and power, and freedom, seemed to depart – the Catholic truths which it maintained, to become changed, distorted, crippled; nay, that the maxims which it introduced upon subjects with which it appeared to have no natural connexion, often contradicted the principles it was commissioned to defend; in other words, that seeking to be all comprehending and circular, it became inefficient and narrow, and roused up that conscience against it, which would else have been most willing to witness in its favour. On these grounds he might arrive at the conviction, that Catholicism cannot exist without Protestantism. He would not mean that Catholicism becomes dangerous when it has not this qualification; he means that it becomes weak, if it have not this support. I say, a person might take this view, and be ready – probably, many are ready – to maintain it on historical grounds. And if he did this, I do not see how Dr. Hook could drive him from his position by the *ipse dixit*, '*We must* become party men.' He might answer, 'so far as I see at present, I cannot be a party man; I cannot be so unjust to either of these schools. I cannot so injure the Protestant school, as to set it up against the Catholic; or so injure the Catholic, as to set it up against the Protestant'.

But a student who takes this ground, is not bound to defend it by any such arguments as those at which I have hinted. Leaving history and reasoning out of the question, he may say '*This is the actual position which is given me by the English Church, and which she bids me keep*.' Do you ask for the proof? I turn to the purely Protestant or Evangelical school, and I find its members working hard to explain away the meaning of our Catholic formularies. 'The Baptismal Service does not *quite* mean this.' The Catechism says, 'that being baptized, we are members of Christ, children of God, inheritors of the kingdom of heaven; but these words must be understood in a peculiar sense.' I do not say that those who take this course now, or who took it in former times, ought to be called Jesuits. I do not think so. I think that some of them were as honest, conscientious men, as ever lived upon this earth. I do not believe they clung to the Church because they could not consent to give up the respectability which it confers; I believe many of them would have been inclined by their peculiar tempers to give up that respectability – to court obloquy and contempt – and that they clave to the Church from principle, and from love, preferring the less contradiction of assenting to forms which they did not heartily agree in, to what struck them as the greater, more practical contradiction of making a schism. I do not wish that they had left the Church. I rejoice that such valuable members of it could contrive to abide in it. But I do not the more for this envy their position. I do not the less for this rejoice that I can receive these formularies in their simple sense, and can feel and give God thanks that that sense pervades the whole liturgy.

I turn again to the Catholic school. I find the most accomplished and logical of its members working hard to explain away the meaning of that formulary which the Reformation bequeathed to us, and in which the Protestantism of that age is, as I and most other persons believe, embodied. He thinks that this may not mean what it seems to mean; it is susceptible of another possible interpretation. Well! I do not call this commentator a Jesuit. I believe of him, as I believe of Mr. Scott or Mr. Newton – that he is perfectly conscientious, thoroughly self-denying, ready to give up anything for the sake of his principles. So far from charging him with a dishonest intention in this particular matter, it seems to me that he has followed out more strictly, and to more unpopular results, than any other member of his school, the maxim which they hold in common, – that Catholicism, though entirely different from and even opposed to Romanism, is nevertheless to supersede Protestantism. I do not believe that he or they cleave to the Church of England from any other motive than a feeling of deep attachment and reverence, and a high sense of duty. I earnestly hope and trust that they may be able to continue in it always. I believe that would be a most sad day for us which took them from us. But because I say this, I am not bound to envy their position. I am not bound to acknowledge myself the disciple of those who think that the Articles which I have subscribed and accepted as the text-book of my studies and teaching, need to be reduced to the minimum of meaning, any more than to be the disciple of those who would oblige me to impart to the Prayer-book, which I have accepted as the guide of the devotions of myself and of my flock, a sense which seems to me equally at variance with its letter and its spirit. But these are the two bodies between which I am to make my election. Under one or other of these, Dr. Hook tells me, I must range myself.

There is yet another point which I would touch upon before I conclude. I cannot submit to Dr. Hook's judgment, greatly as I respect it, upon a matter which concerns my own duty and responsibility; but possibly there may be no better authority respecting the school to which he has attached himself, and of which he is so distinguished an ornament. He declares that this school is, and must be considered, henceforth a *party*. I am deeply concerned to hear it. I believe it is a school which has done great good, and some harm; from this time I greatly fear, if these words be true, the good will become weaker every day, the harm more powerful. The Evangelical school under its first teachers was perhaps more narrow than it is at present: but what an amount of spiritual strength there was in it; what courage, what self-sacrifice! It became a party; it had its coteries; its consistories; its newspapers. It began to produce an effect; the press said it was so respectable and successful, that notice must be taken of it; the divines clapped their hands, and declared that the Gospel was spreading every where; editors were becoming real believers in troops; the millennium was at hand.

Alas! what a shrivelled thing has this popular successful system become. The holy and pious-minded men who are spoken of as maintaining it, do not really represent it. They are determined not to part with the principles which their forefathers bequeathed them, and which they feel to be necessary to their own spiritual life: but they are by no means certain that these are the only important truths; they wish to acknowledge good men who have started from a different point; they like better to call themselves Churchmen than Evangelicals. But the *system* has become a newspaper, cheap book, lecture machinery; not for propagating certain principles, but for attacking and slandering those who are supposed not to hold them, or to hold others different from them. From such melancholy specimens of the vulgar material force which has superseded the spiritual force, whereby the Evangelicals effected their early triumphs, it was, indeed, a refreshment to turn to some of the words and acts of those who called themselves Anglo-Catholics. Such brave faith in the existence of other powers than those which act upon brutes, of other channels through which they work than state decrees or the changeable breath of public opinion, of another source from which they are derived, than the choice or will of man! Such confessions of sloth and sin taking place of the apologies for both which had been called good Churchmanship! Such hearty sympathy with the poor – such courageous, unselfish willingness to bear the reputation of selfishness in the defence of institutions which were established as witnesses against it! Such zeal for theological learning in a day when it is so commonly despised! These feelings, and the deeds which corresponded to them, may well have won the sympathies of earnest, generous minds, and happily there is a life in them which cannot pass away. But along with the head of gold there have been feet of clay; and as in the former case, it is these that will come into prominence, as soon as ever the name and notion of party shall be fairly adopted by our English Catholics. Already we may see melancholy symptoms of a tendency to seek for strength in vulgar helps and earthly expedients. I do not complain, that persons who a few years ago protested strongly against all ridicule on sacred subjects, should now keep a jester to write articles in their Review on the Religious State of the Poor, or the follies and sins of the Clergy. We may try to believe that where there is some good-humour there is not much ill-nature. But there are some defenders of the cause who have no wit to compensate for their violence and feebleness. Why is it more shocking to read advertisements in a religious newspaper, about a clergyman who will preach justification by faith alone, for six weeks at the sea-side, than to read letters and leading articles in a fashionable newspaper about the Sacraments? Why is the quack machinery of the age less offensive, when it is employed in support of 'Catholic Consent,' than when it is used to support the principles of the Bible? But when was a party ever able to disclaim those who resort to these weapons? When has it ever been able to prevent them from acquiring supremacy? The talkers in streets and clubs, for all the purposes of a party, must be more important than the men who live in closets, and keep lonely vigils. And what is more sad, the first do exert an influence over the others: there is a pressure from without to which they unconsciously yield; their pure and noble thoughts take a taint from the vulgar men who call themselves by their names, and bedaub them with their flattery; their big manly voices shrink into childish treble; what they uttered truly in a spiritual sense, is translated by those who hear them, possibly even by themselves, into an earthly sense; and by this most natural process, Catholicism passes now, as it did in former days, into Romanism.

That this dreadful calamity may be averted from this generation, should surely, my dear Mr. Archdeacon, be our constant effort and prayer. I do believe that it will be averted; I do believe that God is preparing some of his servants in the furnace of affliction, that they may be instruments in averting it. Party in both its forms, as opposing Catholicism, and assuming to exalt it, is, I believe, that against which they will have to struggle in themselves, and in the world. If I can do nothing against it, I may at least by these few words stir up others to think whether they must necessarily bind themselves with its fetters. I do not ask anyone to shake them off by deserting the school to which his education or a feeling of his own necessities has attached him. I believe in that school God has meant him to learn, at all events, his first lesson; and that if he learns that lesson humbly and diligently, all others that are good for him will be taught him. I only protest against that loss of humility and diligence which it seems to me inevitably ensues, when we begin to fancy that we are sent into the world to rob other men of their principles, and not to defend our own. It has been painful to me to write what I have written, because I feel that I am censuring men very far wiser and holier than myself. But it is a comfort to me, that I am writing to one whose kindness will impute my presumption to a right motive, who has an ecclesiastical right to correct me, if I am in error, and whose name carries with it a witness that the spirit of party may be defied, even in a region in which it is usually thought to be omnipotent.

RFNJPC, pp. 7–23

On episcopacy as an essential feature of the Anglican approach to church unity.

. . . Supposing it were proposed to us by a body of Lutheran or Calvinistic ministers, that because we are Protestants, because we object to the Church of Rome, because we hold those doctrines respecting personal justification which the Reformers held, we should, therefore, recognise their congregations as organised and rightly constituted bodies, and should as such enter into fellowship with them – I think that according to the principles which I have laid down, we are bound to reject such an invitation. I should express the rejection in some such terms as these: 'That which is the bond of fellowship with the Christians of other nations, must be something which is not national, nor individual, but universal. If we make individual life the foundation of union, we set that up in place of Christ, we substitute our own Election for the Righteousness and Holiness of Christ. We cannot unite as Christians upon a national principle, though it may be a great duty, as Christians, to uphold national life – for it is in its nature exclusive. Now Bishops being as we believe the witnesses and representatives of Christ's universal kingdom, are the very instruments of our communion with other nations. If there be no such institution – no apostleship – in the Church now, then the Church has lost its universal character; then the idea of the Church as existing for all space and all time, perishes; then the commission, "Go ye into all nations,"[4] has no persons to whom it is directed. We cannot then recognise a Church without Bishops. We cannot do it for our own sakes, because we believe that we have a solemn trust and responsibility to uphold this great universal institution of Episcopacy; because we believe that it has been preserved to us in a wonderful manner for the last three centuries, when there was scarcely anything in our minds to make its meaning intelligible; because we believe that all the circumstances of this age are declaring to us its purpose and its necessity.'

TLRWP, pp. 34–5

On the liturgy as a defence against partisanship.

. . . If we use the Prayer Book, not that we may worship God, but that we may lay snares for men, I am sure that it will prove our curse and our damnation. I am greatly afraid of heresy, but I believe it is most prevalent amongst those who are ever on the search for it; who are continually denying some portion of truth in their eagerness to convict their brethren of denying some other portion of it. I claim the Prayer Book and Articles both, as the protection for those who repudiate the parties into which our Church is divided, from their common assaults. I claim them for the protection of these parties from the ferocity of each other. I claim them as a protection of the Truth from their distractions and mutilations. But most of all, dear brethren, I claim this Prayer Book as a witness against your sins and mine.

PBLP, pp. 13–14

Notes

1 This is an oblique reference to the 'Caroline' divines, the seventeenth-century Anglican writers such as Lancelot Andrewes (1555–1626), Jeremy Taylor (1613–67), and George Bull (1634–1710), who were hailed by the Tractarians as forerunners.

2 Cf. E. B. Pusey, *A Letter to the Bishop of Oxford* (1839).

3 Benjamin Hoadly (1676–1761), a 'low church' bishop controversial for his advocacy of the subordination of Church to the State; Thomas Scott (1747–1821), an earnest Evangelical Anglican and co-founder of the Church Missionary Society. Hoadly, though 'low' in his views of the Church, was no Evangelical – hence Maurice's point here.

4 Cf. Matthew 28.19.

11

Social Theology

One of Maurice's most distinctive, and lasting, contributions to Anglican theology was his insistence that the gospel was addressed to society as a whole as much as it was to individuals, and that the responsibility of Christians everywhere was jointly to contribute to the realization of Christ's Kingdom on earth. This was the real heart of his 'Christian Socialism', which arose from his concern that the Church should fulfil its national vocation, rather than from economic theory. Texts chosen here illustrate various aspects of these themes, beginning with his insistence in 1848, the year of revolutions, that religion cannot be separated from the fields of politics, economics and social life.

The prospectus of Politics for the People, *the journal founded by Maurice, Charles Kingsley and John Ludlow in 1848, and Maurice's 'Address' to working men which followed it.*

It is proposed in this Paper to consider the questions which are most occupying our countrymen at the present moment, such as the Extension of the Suffrage; the relation of the Capitalist to the Labourer; what a Government can or cannot do, to find work or pay for the Poor. By considering these questions, we mean that it is not our purpose to put forth ready-made theories upon them, or vehement opinions upon one side or the other. We think that whatever a great number of our countrymen wish for, deserves earnest reflection. It should be studied in the light of present experience and past history. There is leisure for deliberation now, – a year hence there may not be.

To speak of these questions calmly is a duty; to speak of them coldly is a sin; for they cannot be separated from the condition of men who are suffering intensely. If we do not sympathize with their miseries we are not fit to discuss the remedies which they propose themselves, or which others have proposed for them. That sympathy we desire to cultivate in ourselves and in our countrymen. It will be strongest when it is least maudlin. The poor man wishes to be treated as a brother, not to be praised as an angel. Those who flatter him do not love him.

Politics have been separated from household ties and affections – from art, and science, and literature. While they belong to parties, they have no connection with what is human and universal; when they become POLITICS FOR THE PEOPLE, they are found to take in a very large field: whatever concerns man as a social being must be included in them.

Politics have been separated from Christianity; religious men have supposed that their only business was with the world to come; political men have declared that the present world is governed on entirely different principles from that. So long as politics are regarded as the conflicts between Whig, and Tory, and Radical; so long as Christianity is regarded as a means of securing selfish rewards, they will never be united.

But POLITICS FOR THE PEOPLE cannot be separated from Religion. They must start from Atheism, or from the acknowledgment that a Living and Righteous God is ruling in human society not less than in the natural world. Those who make that acknowledgment from their hearts will not proclaim it for the sake of bringing home the charge of infidelity to other men; but that they may apply the highest and severest test to their own thoughts, and words, and actions. The world is governed by God; this is the rich man's warning; this is the poor man's comfort; this is the real hope in the consideration of all questions, let them be as hard of solution as they may; this is the pledge that Liberty, Fraternity, Unity, under some conditions or other, are intended for every people under heaven.

WORKMEN OF ENGLAND,

We who have started this Paper are not idlers in the land, and we have no great sympathy with those that are. But we do not work with our hands; we are not suffering hardships like many of you. Therefore you may think that we shall not understand you. Possibly we shall not altogether at first, but you can help us. Many of you write clearly and nobly; you can tell us what you are thinking and wherein we have mistaken you.

Many people try to convince you that it is in your interest not to injure the richer classes, and to convince them that it is their interest to redress your wrongs. We, who do not, properly speaking, belong to your body or theirs, shall not try to make out that our interests are in common with either. But we believe that we have a DUTY to both, and that you have a DUTY to your own class, to every other, to God. We believe that every true Englishman had rather a thousand times hear his sense of duty spoken to than his self-interest; if any are of a different mind we shall not humour them, for we will not degrade a man in order to get his good will.

We hope not to forget your different occupations; but we wish above all things to remember that you are MEN. To be husbands, fathers, brothers, dwellers on the English soil, children of God, is the inheritance of all classes. Whatever knowledge is fit for men, as men, is fit for you. You have hearts and heads which can take it in, and can give back more than they receive. You are in contact with the realities of life; you can help to make all our studies and thoughts more real.

PFP, no. 1, 6 May 1848, pp. 1–2

Liberty is a Christian ideal. Maurice here writes himself (as 'Editor') into a dialogue between a French propagandist, the editor, and an English labourer.

Frenchman. I hear that you have boasted that you know more of Fraternity than we do.
Editor. Indeed, you are mistaken. I lamented that we know so little of it.
Fr. But you think you, and not we, are in the right road to it.
Ed. There are many roads to it, and a good many of us English may be walking away from it, instead of towards it.
Fr. I do not wish to be rude, but I own it seems to me that you are – a *great* many of you. But my friend here is more interested about another word in our motto. He thinks that you have been reading it backwards. We must be free, he says, before we can be brothers.
Ed. He is right; and the sentiment is a brave, honest, English one.
Fr. So you always say. If we are to believe you, England is THE free nation of the earth.
Ed. Not *me*, my good sir. I never talked in that way.
English Labourer. But you think it, sir. All people of your class do.
Ed. What is my class, my friend? The class of editors? Of all men they have the least pretension to call themselves free. They are a set of hard-worked, over-driven slaves. And as for England generally, I should never boast of its freedom. It might be a free country; it ought to be. I wish I could say it is.
Fr. Come, that is something to grant. We thought you were perfectly

contented with your condition, and wished to make everyone else so.
Ed. I am not at all contented with our condition, and don't wish to make anyone else so.
Fr. Would it not be worth while, in that case, just to try Republican institutions? As long as people are comfortable, there is no hope of their making any effort for something better; but if you are, as you say, ill at ease, you will be as ready to listen to me as my friend here.
E Lab. If you wish for a change, you cannot wonder that *I* should, sir.
Ed. I do not wonder at all. I think, and rejoice to think, that you working men may be the great instruments in bringing it about.
E Lab. So our French friend has been telling me. You must not, he says, wait for the gentlemen to help you in making you free. You must do it for yourselves.
Ed. I go a step further, and think you may help the gentlemen to become free.
Fr. They must cease to be gentlemen if they will have the freedom working men are looking for.
Ed. A gentleman and a freeman used to mean almost the same thing.
Fr. Yes, when all other people were slaves.
Ed. Perhaps. But I don't see why the gentleman should give up his own noble title when other people begin to share it with him.
Fr. What will he care for it, if it is no longer a distinction?
Ed. If he knows what freedom means, what it is to be a gentleman, he will love his honours all the more.
E Lab. And what does freedom mean in the gentleman's language, sir?
Ed. Just what it means in the working man's language, for we, thank God, all speak the same tongue; it means the power of thinking, speaking, acting with the fewest hindrances possible. Is not that the sense you give it? . . .
Fr. Let the Greeks be right or wrong, these suffering men want to be free, and not merely to be told what people, ages ago, thought was the way of becoming so – which way, it seems, did not succeed.
Ed. I quite agree with you; unless we can do more than that, we had better hold our tongues.
Fr. Especially as all your other teaching is just the opposite of this. Your parsons tell the English people, as our priests told the French, till they became suddenly enlightened on the 24th of February last, that they ought not to dream of Liberty as the heathens did, but to be content with servitude as the Bible commands them to be.
Ed. If our parsons or your priests talk in that way, they show that they have never read the book which they profess to reverence. For instance,

they cannot ever have looked into the Book of Exodus, which tells us how the Jews became a nation, and which explains all the after history. For it says, they could not be a nation till they were delivered out of the yoke of bondage; that God was their deliverer and their king; that whenever they followed their animal tendencies they became slaves; that God gave them power to live as men and as citizens. . . We are Christians, therefore we believe that what the Jews held to be true of one nation, is true of all.

Fr. And yet your Christian Knights and Cavaliers, and, in later ages, your Christian merchants and tradesmen, have been holding down the masses, and keeping them as far from themselves as possible.

Ed. Knight means *servant*; *cavalier* means *horseman*. The two words explain the two principles which have been fighting in Christendom these many centuries. I am a servant of Christ and the weak, said the knight. I ride on horseback, he said again, what despicable scoundrels are these that cannot manage a steed and must tramp it on foot! The one was the feeling of the high and brave Christian gentleman – the source of good and gracious deeds – a proclamation of the dignity of all human creatures. The other was the feeling of the man accidentally lifted above his fellows, the source of rude insults to Puritans and Roundheads, by wassailers flushed with insolence and wine – of battles with snobs at the universities – of vulgar refinement, exclusiveness, contempt, profligacy, class legislation, emptiness of brain, hollowness of heart in full-grown aristocrats. The two feelings have come down to the next class. There is the brave, noble, enterprising man, who is occupied with merchandise – the kind-hearted, friendly, devout citizen, who is engaged in trade; there is the mere merchant and the mere tradesman – the worshipper of gold, who is striving with all his nerve to push into a circle, the members of which thrust him back, or else make him pay unconscionable dues for permitting him to be the object of their ridicule – the man who gives wealth, heart, conscience, daughters, to buy lands and titles; the man who must draw out of the workman the tributes which he pays to the superior lords. Which of these habits of mind shall prevail? I believe the answer rests in a great measure with the English working man. He, too, must cultivate one or the other. He must obey those who tell him that the great hardship of all is that he cannot ride in a coach and wear fine clothes; who tell him to spend his life in struggling for prizes which after all he cannot win. Or he must lift up his voice and say, 'This is my complaint of you, gentlemen, tradesmen, whatever you call yourselves – not that you have many things which I have not, but that you have cared so little for that which I have in common with you; that you have not laboured more to make me feel and know that I am a man, and so to make me your fellow-citizen. I demand this recognition of you! I demand this help of you! Refuse it to me, and you refuse it to yourselves. Say you will not deal with me as a man, and you will soon cease to be men yourselves; you will become more emasculated and contemptible in the sight of the nations; we shall soon cease to be a nation. That this may not be, we workmen determine that we will ask strength from God to assert our privileges as men; to prove that we are not animal, to cast aside all the false and degrading doctrines and doctors, who would make us so.

PFP, no. 4, 27 May 1848, pp. 49–52

On the origins of the Book of Common Prayer.

. . . [The Reformers knew] they could treat men – not a few here and there with special tastes and tempers of mind – not easy men with plenty of leisure for self-contemplation – but the poorest no less than the richest, the busiest no less than the idlest, as spiritual beings, with spiritual necessities, with spiritual appetites, which God's Spirit is ever seeking to awaken, and the gratification of which, instead of unfitting them for the common toil of life is precisely the preparation for it, precisely the means of enabling them to be clear, straightforward, manly; to fulfil their different callings in the belief that each one of them, be it grand or petty, sacred or secular in the vocabulary of men, is a holy calling in the sight of God. But to assert that man is a spiritual being in this sense, you must claim for him a right and power to pray – you must give him a common prayer – *common prayer* in every sense of the word, not *special* prayers adapted to special temperaments and moods of character, but human; not refined and artificial, but practical; reaching to the throne of God, meeting the daily lowly duties of man. If our spiritual people will have their spirituality to themselves, if they do not like to acknowledge that all men have spirits, if they think that they bring a set of spiritual feelings with them, when they should come to be quickened and renewed by God's Spirit, they must go empty away. 'Blessed are the poor in spirit, for theirs is the kingdom of Heaven.'[1]

PBLP, pp. 11–12

The earthly presence of the Kingdom of God.

'Blessed are ye that hunger now: for ye shall be filled. Blessed are ye that weep now: for ye shall laugh. But woe unto you that are rich: for ye have received your consolation. Woe unto you that are full: for ye shall hunger. Woe unto you that laugh now: for ye shall mourn and weep.'[2] Language so explicit as this cannot be evaded. And I hold it is greatly for the interest of all of us who are leading easy and comfortable lives in the world that it should not be evaded. If any amount of riches, greater or smaller, does give us consolation, it is well for us to understand that there is a woe upon those riches. They were not meant to give consolation; we were not meant to find it in them. If any laughter of ours does make us incapable of weeping, incapable of entering into the sorrow of the world in which we are dwelling, we ought to feel that there is misery and death in that laughter. Our Lord does not speak against laughter; He sets it forth as a blessing. He does denounce all that laughter which is an exultation in our own prosperity and in the calamities of others. He does promise that those who are indulging that sort of laughter shall weep. I use the word *promise* advisedly. It is a promise, not a threatening; or, if you please, a threat which contains a promise. It is the proof that we are under a kingdom of heaven that God does not allow such laughter to go on; that He stops it; that He gives the blessing of sorrow in place of it. And thus all alike are taught that they are under this fatherly government. All are shewn that the Father in heaven is aware of the discipline which they need, and will apportion it. All may be brought to take their places with their brethren in this kingdom. All may be taught that the common blessings – the blessings from which one cannot exclude another – are the highest blessings. All may be brought to know that this one fact, that they have a Father in heaven, is worth all others. And so that poverty of spirit, which is only another name for childlike dependence upon One who is above us and is all good, because we have found we cannot depend upon ourselves, may be wrought by Him with whom we have to do in poor and rich equally. The heavenly treasures may be revealed to both, which moth and rust cannot corrupt, and which thieves cannot break through and steal.

GKH, pp. 113–14

Why the title 'Christian Socialism' was apt.

To John Malcolm Ludlow, 1850.

I see it clearly. We must not beat about the bush. What right have we to address the English people? We must have something special to tell them, or we ought not to speak. 'Tracts on Christian Socialism' is, it seems to me, the only title which will define our object, and will commit us at once to the conflict we must engage in sooner or later with the unsocial Christians and the unchristian Socialists. It is a great thing not to leave people to poke out our object and proclaim it with infinite triumph. 'Why, you are Socialists in disguise.' '"In disguise;" not a bit of it. There it is staring you in the face upon the title page!' 'You want to thrust in ever so much priest craft under a good revolutionary name.' 'Well, did not we warn you of it? Did we not profess that our intended something was quite different from what your Owenish lecturers meant?'[3] This is the fair play which English people like, and which will save us from a number of long prefaces, paraphrases, apologetical statements which waste time when one wants to be getting to business.

Life, II, pp. 34–5

Christian Socialism as Maurice understands it is not a device for organizing collective action

To Ludlow again, 12 March 1850.

. . . God's order seems to me more than ever the antagonist of man's systems; Christian Socialism is in my mind the assertion of God's order. Every attempt, however small and feeble, to bring it forth I honour and desire to assist. Every attempt to hide it under a great machinery, call it Organisation of Labour, Central Board, or what you like, I must protest against as hindering the gradual development of what I regard as a divine purpose, as an attempt to create a new constitution of society, when what we want is that the old constitution should exhibit its true functions and energies.

For that distinction I exist only to testify. The sooner God pleases that I shall finish my testimony for it, and that some other and more faithful and more wise protestant shall appear, the less will be my sorrow. For having considered and tried to count the cost, I see this only before me, ever increasing misunderstanding, ever increasing incapacity of being a fellow-worker even while I desire to be that and nothing else. To guide and govern is not my business. . . I will with God's help continue to declare in your ears, and in the ears of the half-dozen who are awake on Sunday afternoons, that no Privy Councils, National Councils, or Ecumenical Councils ever did lay, or ever can lay, a foundation for men's souls and God's Church to rest upon. That is what I said in my sermon. I did affirm distinctly that Christ had used councils and might use them when and how He pleased, as He may, for aught I know, construct central boards for the management of trade fraternities. But I do say that neither the Council nor the Central Board can make the fraternity, or establish the law or principles of it, and that if we build churches upon the decrees of councils, or associations upon decrees of central boards, we build upon the sand, and that when the rain comes our houses will fall, and great will be the fall of them.

Life, II, pp. 44–5

Law and economics are dangerous unless they rest on theology.

Benevolent men wish that the poor should know more of Legislation and Ethics and Economy. I wish heartily that they should. But I believe that you will never bring them to that knowledge unless you can point them to the deeper springs of humanity, from which both Ethics and Laws and Economics must be fed, if they are to have any freshness and life. I do not think it dangerous that any man should get any knowledge of any subject whatever; the more he has the better. And I often think that what is sincerely communicated to him of Economics or Physics may bring him sooner to a right moral condition, – may startle him into apprehensions respecting his own being, sooner, – than insincere theological teaching. But yet I cannot help seeing also, that Legislation, Ethics, Economics, even Physical Science, may themselves contribute to the foundation of superstitions, if the man is not first called into life to receive them and to connect them with himself. I am sure, at all events, that an infinite responsibility rests upon us, – not to be interfering with other men, or to be checking their efforts, whatever direction they may take, – but to be calling forth, by that power which, I believe, we possess, if we will use it, the heart and conscience of men, so that being first able to see their Father in heaven truly, and themselves in their true relation to Him, they may afterwards manfully investigate, as I am sure they will long to do, the conditions under which they themselves, His children, exist, and the laws which govern all his works.

TE, pp. 24–5

Notes

1 Cf. Matthew 5.3.

2 Luke 6.2 & 23–4.

3 'Owenish' is a reference to those who followed the doctrines of Robert Owen (1771–1858), the philanthropist and Socialist.

12

Prayer

When Maurice wrote about prayer, it was usually in the context of the prayer of the Church. Both then, and when he wrote at other times about an individual's prayer, it is difficult to escape the conclusion that he had in view something like an epistemological function for prayer, in which the articulation of our human desires and fears connects to the knowledge God has implanted in us, and to the yearning we have for him. Public prayer – the liturgy – stands for Maurice powerfully as a symbol of common humanity before God, and it is therefore a challenge to selfishness. Once again, the principle of comprehensiveness – the breadth of the providence of God – is not far from the surface.

The practice of public prayer is a check to the temptation to reduce prayer to a state of mind and to selfish petitions.

We commence our petitions with the Lord's prayer. This frequent repetition of a formulary which we are told was given merely as a guide for our devotions is, I need not tell you, very offensive to certain critics, and no wonder; for to be reminded by words of our Lord's himself, that prayers are not good in virtue of their seeming application to particular circumstances and conditions of feeling, but are good in virtue of their universality, – this must be very painful to those who have proposed to themselves the former merit as the highest after which they can aspire. We, on the contrary, feeling that we are in continual danger of falling into selfish and peculiar trains of desire and thought, can never be thankful enough for the blessing of being reminded continually what we have need to wish for ourselves and all our brethren. We, too, regard it least as a model, and not as a substitute for other prayer, but we do not feel that there is anything very strange in wishing to have a model constantly before our eyes, nor are we sufficiently convinced of the success of the imitations which have been made of it, by those who think the use of the mere words a bondage, as to believe that we may safely venture upon the same experiment . . .

. . . But what I would chiefly wish you to observe is, that this art is employed, not in contriving expressions for different peculiar circumstances, such as you find noted with painful and impoverishing minuteness in books of Romish, and, I must add, of sectarian devotion generally, – but in leading the spirit to springs of feeling and hope, which lie deepest within the heart of each man, and have a human not a selfish source. In his sudden ejaculations the worshipper is taught to ask for mercy to his race, for blessings on his sovereign, for peace to his land, for the presence of the Spirit in the church. In his more solemn and continuous exercises of thought, each of these desires expands, and a multitude of reflections respecting the character of God and his relations to man grow up by the side of it, till it becomes identified with those wishes which had all along secretly sustained it for the glory of God, and the coming of his kingdom, and the doing of his will. And hence I believe it has come to pass, that there is a clearness and concentration in these thoughts which is wholly wanting in most modern compositions assuming the name of prayers . . .

May not these remarks be some help to us in settling that question respecting answers to prayer, which has given rise to as many irreverent speculations on one side as on the other. If we once admit, that that is most really prayer which is most human and universal, we shall be in no danger of falling into the notion, openly propounded by several writers in the last century, and secretly received by so many others, that prayer is valuable only for its reaction upon the mind of the worshipper. It is barely possible to conceive a notion more affronting to common honesty and truth, and yet one which has more plausibility to a mind that has been tormented by thoughts of its own, or stories of others respecting the blessings which God bestows upon the faithful suppliant. These human blessings being conceived as the greatest that man can ask or God bestow, the very highest idea we can form of the efficacy of prayer is, that they should be granted. To believe that there shall be daily supplies of grace according to our need; that the King shall be supported upon his throne,[1] and that the minister shall be endowed with powers from on high, and that the whole Church shall be sustained in its warfare with the world, and flesh, and devil, is most marvellous. Yet to believe that without prayer these would not be received; that we should not have strength to govern our tempers, to check our desires, to serve others and to love them; that the throne of the King would not be established in righteousness, but that dissension, misery, confusion, would be spread over the land; that the priests would become ungodly, and that the people would perish by their means, – this is not hard for a reasonable man; seeing it is confirmed by his own experience, and by the experience of history. Answers to prayer, then, and those of the most startling and amazing kind, we believe that we are every day meeting with; and why, then, do we object to the language which some use upon this subject, and to the expectation which it excites? Is it because God takes no care of particular persons, and of their interests? Is it because we think it too mean a thing for him to cause that this man should have money to pay a debt, or that man should be preserved when his horse stumbles? By no means; we attribute all these events, down to the fall of a sparrow, to the ever-present superintendence of God; and surely it would be most inconsistent for us to object to any confidence in that fatherly providence or any acts which it may generate. But we do object to that mode of training men to observe this care and providence of God, which has a tendency to fix them in selfishness, instead of leading them on to love; which has a tendency to make them think of themselves in the first place, and of God in the second place; which has a tendency to make spiritual thoughts and hopes the ministers to narrowness and secularity.

KC, 1st edn, II, pp. 240–4

The same theme developed.

All our previous remarks have tended to show, that prayer is emphatically, the deliverance of a man out of his selfishness. It would have been easy, therefore, to have used the very language of your writers, and to have spoken of the man himself as being lost in the act of prayer; but in so doing I should have deceived you. It is one thing to speak as if the worshipper were a mere passive instrument; it is the most opposite thing possible, to teach that all his energies and activities are moving towards an object, in which they must finally repose. This, I conceive, is precisely the difference between the mystical faith and the Catholic faith. Mysticism seeks its Sabbath in that annihilation of personal feeling, which it supposes to be the result of submission to the Divine Spirit; the Catholic doctrine teaches that the Spirit rouses each man into personal consciousness and life, leads him to connect that life with the life of his kind, and gives him his full enjoyment and satisfaction only when he can behold God as the resting-place of their hopes as well as his own. Mysticism contemplates the whole human race only as it affects the condition of the individual, – we are to be kind, gentle, charitable to our fellow men lest we should disturb the balance of our own spirits;

Catholicism contemplates the individual only as he is a member of the race which is constituted by God in Christ. Mysticism, therefore, is always forgetting that Christ is a Mediator, in order that it may exalt him as a quickening Spirit, – it loses sight of God as an absolute Being, and regards only his acts and influences upon the man; the Catholic Church looks upon the Spirit as given that he may testify of the Father and the Son, – as leading men to behold the Mediator, and in him to worship and glorify the one living and true God, the Father, the Son, and the Holy Ghost. Mysticism only recognizes the idea of a Trinity, because certain acts and feelings of ours can be explained on no other hypothesis; the Catholic Church regards it as a mystery which is surrounding and encompassing man in all his journey through earth, and the fruition which shall be his great reward when the darkness is past, and when in God's light we shall see light.

KC, 1st edn, II, pp. 247–9

Prayer can carry us through the torment of doubt, without abolishing doubt.

To the Revd J. De la Touche, 14 April 1863.

How, you ask, can I use the prayers of the Church which assume Christ's divinity when I cannot see sufficient proof that He is Divine. That is a question, it seems to me, which no man can answer for you; nay, which you cannot answer for yourself. If I am right, it is in prayer you must find the answer. Yes, in prayer to be able to pray; in prayer to know what prayer is; in prayer to know whether, without a mediator, prayer is not a dream and an impossibility for you, me, every one. I cannot solve this doubt. I can but show you how to get it solved. I can but say, the doubt itself may be the greatest blessing you ever had, may be the greatest striving of God's Spirit within you that you have ever known, may be the means of making every duty more real to you . . .

Life, II, p. 446

In prayer, we are brought into the very presence of God himself, and guided by him.

[T]hus you will be able to understand the sense of the last words in the collect. 'That, Thou being our ruler and guide, we may so pass through things temporal, that we finally lose not the things eternal.'[2] You cannot think that all this wonderful and mysterious guidance is for nothing; you cannot think that the creature who requires it is made only to maintain a hard fight with a set of cruel enemies and then to perish. There must be things eternal, and we must be meant to share in them. But what are they, and where are they, and when may we hope to enter into possession of them? Mark the words. The prayer supposes that in some sense they are ours now; for it speaks of our losing them; it asks that they may not be taken from us. And this is the language of the New Testament. 'He hath given unto us eternal life,' saith St. John, 'and this life is in his Son.'[3] Which words would be strange and unintelligible to us, if they were not explained by one greater than St. John. 'This is life eternal, saith our Lord, that they may know Thee, the only true God, and Jesus Christ whom Thou hast sent.'[4] This mighty knowledge has been given to us; the Son of God has brought it near to us. In him we possess it. In him man is taken into the height, and depth, and length, and breadth, of that love, which passeth knowledge.[5] This love enfolds us at our baptism. The name of the Father, and the Son, and the Holy Ghost is the utterance of it. From this Love the images and pictures of this world, the created, temporal things, are seeking to withdraw us. We cannot enjoy them without it; from it alone they borrow their lustre. Yet they would tempt us to forsake it for them; to dwell in them and not in it. The invisible guide of our hearts is drawing them by a thousand gracious acts and influences, and invitations, from the perishable to the eternal; from that which is the likeness of the thing they long for, to the thing itself; from that which loses its beauty when we can no longer give it beauty, to that first source of beauty from which we and they alike draw our life. We pray this week that his power may not be exerted in vain; we pray it for His sake who died that these eternal treasures might be ours, who lives that we may not be defeated of them through our own wilfulness and folly; for the sake of Jesus Christ our Lord.

CDOS, pp. 350–1

Notes

1 This passage was written before the death of William IV in 1837.

2 This is a quotation from the collect for the Fourth Sunday after Trinity, in the Book of Common Prayer.

3 Cf. 1 John 5.11.

4 Cf. John 17.3.

5 Cf. Ephesians 3.18.

Select Bibliography

Main works by F. D. Maurice

Subscription no Bondage, or the practical advantages afforded by the Thirty-Nine Articles as guides in all the branches of academical education, Oxford, 1835

The Kingdom of Christ, or Hints on the Principles, Ordinances, and Constitution of The Catholic Church in Letters to a Member of the Society of Friends, 3 vols, 1838; new edn, 2 vols, 1842

Reasons for not joining a party in the Church: A Letter to the Ven. Samuel Wilberforce, 1841

Three Letters to the Revd W. Palmer, 1842

The Epistle to the Hebrews, 1846

Moral and Metaphysical Philosophy, published in 4 parts, 1847–73

The Religions of the World and their Relations to Christianity, 1847

The Lord's Prayer: Nine sermons, 1848

Politics for the People (a weekly journal), 6 May 1848–29 July 1848

The Prayer-Book considered especially in reference to the Romish System: Nineteen Sermons, 1849 (later combined with 'The Lord's Prayer' in *The Prayer Book and the Lord's Prayer*, 1880)

The Church a Family: Twelve Sermons on the Occasional Services of the Prayer-Book, 1850

The Patriarchs and Lawgivers of the Old Testament, 1851

The Prophets and Kings of the Old Testament, 1853

Sermons on the Sabbath-Day, 1853

Theological Essays, Cambridge, 1853

The Word 'Eternal' and the Punishment of the Wicked: A Letter to the Revd Dr. Jelf, Canon of Christ Church and Principal of King's College, Cambridge, 1853

The Doctrine of Sacrifice deduced from the Scriptures, 1854

Learning and Working, Cambridge, 1855

The Gospel of St. John: A Series of Discourses, 1856

Sermons preached in Lincoln's Inn Chapel, 6 vols, 1856–9

What is Revelation? 1859

Sequel to the Inquiry, What is Revelation? 1860

Dialogues between a Clergyman and a Layman on Family Worship, 1862

The Gospel of the Kingdom of Heaven: A Course of Lectures on the Gospel of St. Luke, 1864

The Conscience, 1868

Social Morality, 1869

The Friendship of Books, 1893
The Acts of the Apostle: A Course of Sermons, 1894

Works about Maurice and about his context

Allchin, A. M., 'F. D. Maurice as Theologian', *Theology*, vol. 76, 1973
Allen, P., *The Cambridge Apostles: The Early Years*, Cambridge University Press, 1978
Avis, P., *Anglicanism and the Christian Church: Theological Resources in Historical Perspective*, Fortress Press, 1989
Brose, O. J., *Frederick Denison Maurice: Rebellious Conformist*, Ohio University Press, 1971
Brown, S. J., *The National Churches of England, Ireland and Scotland 1801–1846*, Oxford University Press, 2001
Bryant, C., *Possible Dreams: A Personal History of British Christian Socialists*, Hodder & Stoughton Religious, 1996
Butler, B. C., *The Idea of the Church*, Darton, Longman & Todd, 1962
Chadwick, W. O., *The Victorian Church*, 2 vols, SCM Press, 1966 & 1970
Christensen, T., *The Origins and History of Christian Socialism 1848–1854*, Universitetsforlaget, Aarhus, 1962
Christensen, T., *The Divine Order: A Study of F. D. Maurice's Theology*, E. J. Brill, 1973
Cracknell, K., *Justice, Courtesy and Love: Theologians and Missionaries Encountering World Religions 1816–1914*, Epworth Press, 1995
Flesseman-Van Leer, E., *Grace Abounding: A Comparison of F. D. Maurice and Karl Barth*, King's College London, 1968
Gloyn, C. K., *The Church in the Social Order: A Study of Anglican Social Theory from Coleridge to Maurice*, Pacific University Press, 1942
Gray, D., *Earth and Altar: The Evolution of the Parish Communion in the Church of England to 1945*, Canterbury Press, 1986
Harrison, J. F. C., *A History of the Working Men's College, 1854–1954*, Routledge & Kegan Paul, 1954
Higham, F., *F. D. Maurice*, SCM Press, 1947
Hinchliff, P. B., *God and History: Aspects of British Theology 1875–1914*, Clarendon Press, 1992
Jenkins, C., *F. D. Maurice and the New Reformation*, SPCK, 1938
Jones, P. D'A., *The Christian Socialist Revival 1877–1914: Religion, Class and Social Conscience in Late Victorian England*, Princeton University Press, 1968
Lidgett, J. Scott, *The Victorian Transformation of Theology*, Epworth Press, 1934
McClain, F. M., *Maurice, Man and Moralist*, SPCK, 1972
McClain, F., Norris, R. and Orens, J., *F. D. Maurice: A Study*, Cowley Press, 1982
Maurice, F., *Life and Letters of F. D. Maurice*, 1884
Morris, J. N., *F. D. Maurice and the Crisis of Christian Authority*, Oxford University Press, 2005
Newsome, D., *Two Classes of Men: Platonism and English Romantic Thought*, J. Murray, 1974

Norman, E. R., *The Victorian Christian Socialists*, Cambridge University Press, 1987
Prickett, S., *Romanticism and Religion: The Tradition of Coleridge and Wordsworth in the Victorian Church*, Cambridge University Press, 1976
Ramsey, A. M., *The Gospel and the Catholic Church*, 1936
Ramsey, A. M., *F. D. Maurice and the Conflicts of Modern Theology*, Cambridge University Press, 1951
Reckitt, M. B., *Maurice to Temple: A Century of the Social Movement in the Church of England*, Faber, 1947
Rowell, G., *Hell and the Victorians: A Study of the Nineteenth-Century Theological Controversies concerning Eternal Punishment and Future Life*, Oxford University Press, 1974
Sachs, W. L., *The Transformation of Anglicanism: From State Church to Global Communion*, Cambridge University Press, 1993
Sanders, C. R., *Coleridge and the Broad Church Movement*, Duke University Press, 1942
Sykes, S. W., *The Integrity of Anglicanism*, Mowbray, 1978
Thompson, D. M., 'F. D. Maurice', in S. P. Mews (ed.), *Modern Religious Rebels*, Epworth Press, 1993
Tulloch, J. R., *Movements of Religious Thought in Britain During the Nineteenth Century*, 1885, reprinted Leicester University Press, 1971
Vidler, A. R., *F. D. Maurice and Company: Nineteenth Century Studies*, SCM Press, 1966
Welch, C., *Protestant Thought in the Nineteenth Century: I. 1799–1870*, Wipf & Stock Publishers, 1972
Wilkinson, A., *Christian Socialism: From Scott Holland to Tony Blair*, 1998
Wolf, W. J., Booty, J. E. and Thomas, O. C., *The Spirit of Anglicanism: Hooker, Maurice and Temple*, Moorhouse Publishing Company, 1982
Young, D., *F. D. Maurice and Unitarianism*, Clarendon Press, 1992

Index of Names

Index of Subjects